A HANDBOOK ON
STAFF DEVELOPMENT IN LIBRARIES

A HANDBOOK ON
STAFF DEVELOPMENT IN LIBRARIES

By :

S.K Kapoor

2007

CYBER TECH PUBLICATIONS
4264/3, Ansari Road, Darya Ganj
New Delhi 110002 Ph. : 23244078

A HANDBOOK ON STAFF DEVELOPMENT IN LIBRARIES

S.K Kapoor

First Edition 2007

Published by :

G.S. Rawat for **Cyber Tech Publications**
4264/3, Ansari Road, Darya Ganj, New Delhi 110002

Printed at :

PREFACE

'Knowledge Explosion' and 'information explosion' are the terminologies used to represent the growth of knowledge. Knowledge gets accumulated; process of organizing knowledge available in different formats is the skilled work of knowledge workers. Librarian is the knowledge navigator. His task comprises principles and information technology to develop, deifies and utilize knowledge. Information tools are designed and developed to help the learning process in the education dissemination system.

With the changing technology and their induction in libraries, the librarians have to update their skill to cope with the situation. Hence the need of staff development.

This book addresses some crucial issues pertaining to staff development inn libraries. Hopefully, this handbook will prove of utmost use.

The information is substantially based on secondary sources. I am thankful to all original contributors whose works are liberally borrowed. I appreciate and thank to all who have rendered help and assistance while compiling the material. Finally my publishers deserve my appreciation for bringing out his book in so nice way.

—Author

CONTENTS

1

BASIC PLANNING OF STAFF DEVELOPMENT AND ASSESSING TRAINING

INTRODUCTION TO BASIC PLANNING

The manager's responsibility to help staff to realize their full potential, improving their performance through making the most of their abilities. In many cases the manager may be the person conducting the training, and even if that is not the case, they will almost certainly be evaluating its outcome in day-to-day performance, not only in the period immediately following the training but continuously. Being a manager also implies taking on a much wider role within the organization as a whole, for example as a member of a planning committee. That wider role will help considerably in the management of the training activity for the US. First there will be a range of useful points of reference throughout the organization in the form of other managers who, although running departments with a different specialist focus, are likely to share common areas of responsibility such as staff training and development. There may well be regular managers' meetings, which will act as a focus for such discussion, as well as providing the opportunity to get to know each other and the work of the various departments in much more detail. A second point of reference will be any central department which may exist to serve training needs across the organization. This may be part of the personnel function, which in the absence of a separate training function will also be able to provide useful advice. The personnel department is the one you will be most likely to consult about training policies, training contracts, and any statements about training which may be included in the written conditions of employment sent out to new recruits. These will have set the expectations of new staff as to what will actually happen from their first day of employment.

Having already received answers to the initial questions about organizational guidelines on training, you will now be aware of a number of factors which will have to be taken into account when designing a departmental training programme. Perhaps it would be helpful at this stage to draw up a more detailed management checklist, looking first at in-house policies and facilities by establishing answers to the following questions:

- Is there a central training department?
- Does any single person have overall responsibility for training throughout the organization, and if so, who?
- Is there a central training policy?
- Are policies and procedures set out in any sort of staff manual?
- Is there a central training budget?
- Who controls training expenditure?
- Do departments have separate/supplementary training budgets?
- What sort of in-house courses are available?
- What specialist knowledge can be called on?
- What training skills exist?
- What training facilities and equipment are there?

The answers to such questions should help you to assess whether the existing in-house training facilities and programmes would be relevant, or could be adapted to suit your requirements.

The organizational climate, especially senior management support for, and encouragement of, training and development, will have a strong influence on its successful implementation. The importance of training as perceived by employing organizations, with a number of them setting up central training departments and appointing those responsible for them at a senior, often director, level, and offering increased training opportunities for staff at all levels. A positive organizational climate is also likely to be supportive of the use of appropriate external training. However, as with all expenditure, both of money and of time, it is always up to the individual manager to make the case for it in terms of organizational benefits.

When planning training for a specific department it is important to adopt a coordinated approach, designing an overall training plan which will take into account the present needs of, and future plans for the service (as perceived in relation to the future needs of the organization), while retaining the flexibility essential to be able to meet the often very different needs of each member of staff who may be undergoing training at any one time.

It is essential that all training is carefully planned, from the identification of needs and the ways in which these might be satisfied, to the incorporation of training costs into the budget. Timing is also crucial; first, the individual will need certain training before he or she can progress to the next stage, and secondly the period of time between training sessions needs to be long enough for earlier training to be assimilated and put into practice, but not so long that earlier learning is lost and unable to be built on without further repetition. Training may be task-specific or broader-based, such as that aimed at developing administrative and organizational skills, or relating to the communication and interpersonal aspects of the job. The whole process needs to be structured into a logical sequence for maximum benefit.

With some activities it may be appropriate for several members of staff to undertake training together, as in the case where new procedures or new services are being introduced, such as automated cataloguing, additional online services or a help desk. It is also important to remember that you as manager have to sell the idea of the training, not only to senior management but also to those who are to receive it. They need to be assured that this is a beneficial activity, not a threatening one, and that it is being planned to suit their specific needs. No matter how much training is provided, if the reasons for it are not explained sensitively and in positive terms the training itself is not likely to achieve maximum impact.

It is good practice to involve the individual in the total process-in assessing their own needs, in setting objectives, in talking through alternative training methods as to their appropriateness, and after the event, by encouraging feedback and discussion on each piece of training, not just with you as the manager, but also with other members of the department. This can lead to an enhanced teamwork approach, with the sharing of experience having valuable spin-off in terms of staff relationships and US operations and initiatives. The full value of training is then much more likely to be perceived and the individual more highly motivated to pursue it with enthusiasm and to invest the necessary personal effort. The achievement of training objectives may lead to expectations of rewards, such as promotion, or perhaps a salary increase. It is important that any training programme is therefore developed within the framework of an overall career structure, so that any expectations are clearly based on fact rather than surmise. This is clearly demonstrated in the CSIRO case study.

Some employers, for example, currently offer a bonus on the achievement of Associate or other equivalent professional status. Additional responsibility may not always be regarded strictly as a reward, although most staff would see it as a mark of confidence in their ability and an enhancement of their status, and it could naturally follow the successful outcome of training. This also needs to be built into the initial discussion in planning the training programme, so that in addition to meeting the specific objectives of each training event, the individual will be able to establish other longer-term goals.

The planning of your departmental training may well start with a review of the service and an examination of any staff manual or overall training policy to see what is generally regarded as being essential for all staff. You could then focus on any specialist training provided to other functions or departments. It would be wise before going further to have an open discussion with the training or personnel department about such aspects as, for example, payment of course fees, study leave, day release, and the provision of training materials. This will also provide you with the opportunity to put forward or clarify matters relating specifically to US training and development, for example employer support for initial and continuing professional education, opportunities for the pursuit of paraprofessional qualifications such as the City and Guilds examinations, and what such support might consist of in terms of, say, the provision of study time or the payment of fees. There may also be other general questions that you wish to raise.

How to Get Started?

There are two wonderful attributes inherent in staff development: the initiative for it can come from anyone anywhere in the organization, and the object of it is human growth. Whether that initiative blossoms or withers and whether staff members grow or stagnate depend on how thoughtfully the process toward fulfillment is managed. The questions in this chapter are intended to ensure a thoughtful consideration of the range of issues pertinent to a beginning staff development effort. There are no right or wrong answers to these questions except as they relate to your specific undertaking.

Think Small : The One-Shot Program

1. Is there a particular program/issue of interest to a significant segment of your staff? If no, why do you want a staff-development program? (Maybe something else will address the need.) If yes, which issue(s)? Which staff? How do you know this?

2. What benefit(s) should result? Improved staff morale? New knowledge? Improved performance? Changed performance? Increased effectiveness? Cost savings? What results or outcomes are sought? By whom?

3. Who makes up the target audience?

4. What format is appropriate? Panel discussion with large audience? Workshop with few participants? Film? Single speaker? Seminar? Newsletter? Information-sharing "clinic?" Informal, staff-initiated staff gathering (e.g., bag lunch)? How have others handled the topic?

5. Who should organize it? Administrative task force? Existing staff committee? Ad hoc committee of interested staff within one library unit or among library units?

6. How can administrative support be obtained when it is lacking?

   Have the administrative objections been addressed? Have the expected benefits been articulated sufficiently? Is the maximum staff support for the program evident?

7. How much time should be allotted for preparation? Allow more time (up to six months) the more of the following that apply: contracting for speaker(s) and agreeing on fees and expenses (if any), program date, room requirements, and equipment; scheduling the room and arranging for the setup of the room and special equipment; preparing (writing and designing) handouts; producing and duplicating handouts; handling publicity, pre-enrollment, and confirmation of enrollment; arranging for the presence of a technician to handle on-the-spot technical problems or for an assistant to help with furniture moving and other setup activities the day of the program; arranging for refreshments and lunch; preparing name tags, registration sheets, and evaluation form.

8. Who is eligible to attend? Participants appointed by administration? Voluntary? Maximum attendance allowed? Minimum attendance required?

9. How should the program be publicized? Is program description geared toward the intended audience? Does publicity clearly identify the intended audience?

10. What facilities and equipment are needed? Arrangement of room for lecture? For discussion? Flexible seating for interchanging small and large-group gatherings? Will attendees need writing surfaces? Writing materials? Where to go for breaks? Food? Will speaker's voice carry? Ambience of room: stuffy air? Light enough? Comfortable enough? Can thermostat be adjusted at will? Blackboard? Easels, pens, and masking tape? Projectors (for transparencies, slides, film)? Computer demos? Monitors, modems, phone lines (test them out)? Sufficient electrical outlets?

11. How should the program be evaluated? Were expected benefits derived? How do you know? How will you measure the change (in morale, knowledge, behavior,

etc.) as a result of the program? Was need fulfilled? Is it worth repeating? What mistakes were made? What was left out? What was done especially well?

12. What next? Should a report be written up and distributed? If worth repeating, how often? Should new staff eventually be reached with this program:' If yes, how? Is this the start of something bigger—one of a series on a broader topic?

Developing a Continuing Program

1. Is there agreement about a definition of staff development? Position-related? Career-related? Primary beneficiary: individual? Library? Must enhance or support library goals? Which ones? Does a written policy exist for your organization?

2. Who is doing what for whom? What and whose needs have been identified and assessed? To what extent are these needs already being met? Is there agreement among staff and between staff and administration about the need? In -whole? In part? If no, how can agreement be reached—in whole or in part? Is there agreement about the expected outcome?

3. What types of programs would fulfill the need(s) and achieve the desired outcome(s)? Ones that improve skills? Change behavior? Broaden perspectives? Address issues of immediate concern? How do they match with definition of staff development?

4. Where to find the expert speakers and presenters? Internally? From parent organization (e.g., city, state, campus)? From nearby library? Regional continuing education programs? Library consultants? Recommendations from other libraries? Professional organizations or associations—regional, state, national?

5. Do program presenters have not only expertise in the program topic but also skills in making effective presentations? Can internal staff with knowledge of program topic be given training in oral or written presentation skills to develop in-house presenters?

6. How to promote transfer of learning to on-the-job performance? Establish expectations ahead of time with participants' supervisors? With participants? With program leaders? Ensure continued learning environment on the job (e.g., coaching, practice time)? Plan to follow up to check out expectations?

7. Budget? Costs? Fees for outside speakers? How much for publicity? Refreshments? Facilities rental? Film rental? Handouts? Hidden costs—staff time, things not getting done because of this program? Registration fees and travel funding for external workshops? (Remember to weigh these costs against costs of not doing the program.) What sources of funding? Is cost recovery possible—e.g., external sale of well-developed program materials or jointly sponsored program with nearby library(ies)?

Follow-up

1. Who will be responsible for continued programming? Ensuring a post-program on-the-job learning environment until program objectives are reached? Continued assessment of needs? Adherence to program standards? Advocating adequate funding? Continued evaluation of programs? An individual? A committee? A combination?

2. To what extent will attendance be voluntary versus mandatory?

3. How will follow-up planning occur to ensure skills transfer after each program?

4. Over a one-year period, what new programs will be given? What programs will be repeated? What programs over a two-year period?

5. Over time, who approves allocation of *funds* for staff development? Administration? A balance of administration and staff? How often do the individuals who approve funds change?

6. From where and whom are *ideas* for new programs being solicited? How?

EVALUATION AND MONITORING

It would be helpful at this stage to establish whether there are any centrally designed feedback mechanisms currently in use to evaluate training and development, such as questionnaires or checklists, and to obtain samples of these so that you can feed these requirements into your planning, and also to consider whether such forms need to be adapted for departmental use. They may in fact form part of the organization's appraisal system, and as such be the standard means of evaluation and feedback,

Training and development activities are pursued in order that certain objectives can be met. In planning these you will need to think about their evaluation in terms of their effectiveness in achieving those objectives. This is well illustrated by the Glasgow and CSIRO case studies.

Evaluation can take place in several ways, as follows:

- Participant response via completion of a post-event questionnaire, or a written report or short presentation to other staff about what the event achieved.

- Regular consultation between the manager and the person undergoing the training or development programme.

- Ongoing monitoring of individual performance by the manager through observation or by performance tests which require demonstration of the successful application of the skill or knowledge acquired. Rather than being regarded as a formal academic exercise these ran be incorporated into daily work activities, with the trainee being asked to handle live problems under supervision and with subsequent feedback.

Evaluation and monitoring activities can add another dimension to team-building, but need to be presented in a positive way to staff and handled sensitively. They also need to be well structured so that they provide the information you are seeking and contribute to the ongoing appraisal process. Where problems are identified, prompt management follow-up will be required while the problem is still fresh in the mind of the trainee, otherwise the benefits of other parts of the training may be lost. Swift management action is also important as a sign of the manager's continued interest and overall confidence in the individual concerned.

Some organizations may also require an evaluation of training and development as part of their regular review of recruitment policy, looking to see if there are links between staff turnover and the availability and effectiveness of a staff development programme.

The Training Budget

The personnel or training department may well control a central training budget, which is something else that could influence your own training activities. In the research study *Best practice* approximately half of the participating organizations exercised central control of training budgets, whereas the other half operated departmental training budgets. Another interesting fact which emerged was that even where there were central budgets, these were often viewed as being for general training, e.g. management and business skills required across the organization, with a supplementary budget controlled by departments and intended purely for their specialist needs. The availability of in-house training will influence the planning of your budget, but this should not be the sole factor in determining whether to take up internal opportunities for training or to seek those on offer externally.

It must be remembered that even in-house courses cost money: both the person running the course and those attending it are not available to carry out other work for the period of time during which the training takes place. In some cases an outside lecturer or agency is brought in to design and conduct courses, often charging quite a high fee for doing so. However, the enlightened organization sees such costs as an investment in its own future development, and may also regard them as central and not attributable to particular departments.

On-the-job training also has a cost in terms of staff time-not just the time spent giving the training, but also that required for its preparation. Staff time costs vary not only according to the grade on which each person is paid, but also according to their specific abilities, which may dictate that in some circumstances only one person would be able to carry out a particular task. If that service is required regularly, for example translation, or some other specialist service for which that person's specialist skills are required, it would not be cost-effective for them to be seconded to the training role too frequently. In the case of online training the costs of using each database also need to be taken into consideration, although there are ways of minimizing these. For example, the use of 'live' enquiries in the training process, with the trainee in the passenger seat at first. Also take advantage of the free online time and free or low-priced seminars offered by many database providers and hosts - these can make a useful contribution to the training budget.

Even where there is a central training budget it may still be the case that training specific to your department will be under your control, and shown as just one cost centre within your overall budget. However, you may still find it helpful to breakdown the expenditure, for example by person and/or type of training. This could prove useful in staff planning, recruitment and service development. It might also assist in broader organizational planning. Budgeting for training is part of your overall financial planning but it should be regarded not only as part of the cost of running the library or information service; it also needs to be balanced against the organizational and departmental benefits which accrue from staff development and training.

Angela Bridgeland suggests that, in addition to the direct costs of training, e.g. trainers fees, materials, equipment and administrative costs, managers also have to consider the hidden costs. Among these she notes cost benefits, that is, what would the cost of *not* doing the training be against the direct cost, and, what would be done better as a result of training?

BACIE, the British Association for Commercial and Industrial Education, runs a series of workshops and seminars called Training for Profit. BACIE suggests that this approach will help training managers to use the techniques of financial analysis in order to:

- Relate training to the objectives and competitive strategy of the organization
- Develop training to improve the levels of profitability and financial performance
- Balance training investment between meeting long-term and short-term needs.

Librarians and information managers could well find this approach, which is also described by Darling, useful in helping them to argue the case for training investment, as well as assisting them in the design and implementation of training.

Transfer of training can be enhanced by a few simple procedures performed by the trainer, the participant, and the participant's supervisor. It is important to remember that training will not result automatically in increased ability levels unless some of these additional steps are taken. Depending upon the organization, some steps may be more effective than others.

WHAT THE TRAINER CAN DO

The trainer can take the lead in ensuring transfer. Although the participant and the manager share this responsibility, the trainer is in the best position to encourage transfer strategies.

1. Find out as much as possible about the library or the unit within the library where the training will occur. This advice holds as true for trainers who are part of the organization as it does for those who are hired from the outside. Know what people do, how they are rewarded, and what the goals are.

2. Identify any likely barriers. If resistance is strong, training may fail to produce the desired results.

3. Solicit the interest and support of managers early in the process. Familiarize managers with the concepts and principles of the training program but avoid forcing disinterested managers into playing a more active role.

4. Distribute a set of advance reading materials or assignments to participants. State the training objectives and specify what participants will be expected to do differently following the training session.

5. Test the knowledge of participants beforehand. This process will enlighten the audience as to how much they do not know, which can increase their interest in the program.

6. Train intact groups rather than selecting one individual from each unit. Peer-group support is a major factor in determining whether newly learned skills will transfer.

7. Focus on a few related concepts. Do not go overboard trying to jam too many points into a single session. Depth is more important than breadth.

8. Provide trainees with as much detailed and individualized instruction on how and when to use the new skills as possible. (This requires a certain degree of job knowledge on the part of the trainer.)

9. Allow participants to practice the skills during the training session. If time permits, allow practice beyond the point at which a procedure or skill can be done correctly. One successful attempt is often insufficient to guarantee transfer.

10. Discuss the concept of transfer with the participants.

11. At the end of the session, give the participants appropriate job aids, such as checklists or reference manuals.

12. Arrange for follow-up contacts to provide support and respond to difficulties encountered in the application of the skills. Consider offering a refresher course that deals with the problems of implementation.

13. If the resources are available, consider posttraining evaluation to measure performance improvements.

WHAT THE TRAINEE CAN DO

Employees need to take an active role in their own professional development. When something is missing from the training program, such as a follow-up session, ask if it may be included.

1. When possible, select training programs to meet existing interests and job needs. If a staff-development needs analysis has not been done, participants should suggest specific programs which they think will be useful.
2. Prepare as much as possible before the training session. If materials have not been distributed, ask the trainer to suggest one or two articles which discuss the concepts to be covered in the program.
3. Constantly think of possible on-the-job applications throughout the workshop.
4. Document efforts made between the training program and any follow-up session to use the new skills. Note any difficulties, and plan to share these with the trainer.
5. Refer frequently to course materials, action plans, and training contracts.
6. Form support groups with others who have attended the training session. Discuss strategies and obstacles related to implementation.

WHAT THE MANAGER CAN DO

Perhaps the most overlooked aspect of the training process has been the role of the manager or supervisor. If an employee's supervisor is interested in the training program, expects to see results, and intends to recognize and reward the use of new skills and knowledge on the job, then the chances of transfer are greatly increased.

1. Avoid packaged programs that are too general. Participants have greater difficulty relating to situations that have little to do with their own work.
2. Consider abandoning existing programs which have not resulted in measurable improvement. Ineffective training is not only wasteful, it can be detrimental.

3. Select several employees from a single library unit. This will increase the likelihood that concepts taught in the training session will be discussed back on the job.

4. Initially, send employees who are involved in their jobs and interested in improving their performance. While these individuals may not need the training as much as others, their enthusiasm may help build interest among other employees.

5. Meet with the trainer beforehand to discuss existing problems, relevant examples, and appropriate follow-up strategies. Select a project which will enable employees to use the new skills once they return to work.

6. Preview instructional materials for accuracy and relevance.

7. Become familiar with the skills and terminology which will be covered in the program.

8. Notify employees well in advance of the program. Encourage preparation.

9. Meet with participants before the training begins. Go over the objectives and indicate support for the program.

10. Release trainees from normal duties and distractions during the training period. If possible, arrange for the training to take place outside the library.

11. Meet with participants immediately following the training session. Discuss possible on-the-job applications. Reinforce any effort to use new skills.

12. Arrange for trainees to share their experience with other employees. Make sure that trainees know that they will be expected to do this before they participate in the program.

13. Provide low-risk opportunities for participants to try out their new skills on the job.

14. Arrange for subsequent training to build on skills already learned.

Most of these suggestions require little cost but have great benefit. Think of previous training programs that have taken place in your library. Chances are that most of them could have been improved by adding one or more of these steps. Understanding the concept of transfer and the conditions that impede or promote it will help make training and staff-development programs worthwhile. When you ensure some level of transfer, your training dollars will go farther.

EFFECTIVE PRESENTATION

Every effective presentation has three components: sufficient preparation, competent delivery, and supportive visual aids. This chapter highlights the ingredients that make up the other two components.

Sufficient Preparation

Never underestimate the importance of preparation. "It takes three weeks," Mark Twain once said, "to prepare a good ad-lib speech." Here are the five primary steps of the preparation process:

1. Complete this sentence: "After attending my presentation, my audience will know/know how to/ be able to ...."

2. Define your audience and its need. Who needs to know this information? Why? What prior knowledge is required?

3. Organize your talk around no more than three to four major points.

4. Write a draft. Then rewrite it. Then speak it. To

make an effective presentation, knowing your topic is not enough. There is often a big gap between what you mean to say and what you say. You need to be able to explain what you know so others can understand. Do not rely solely on an outline—it increases the risk of illogical exposition, hazy description of complex ideas, and sloppy digression. Writing your talk does not mean that you must read what you wrote, but it does provide you with a mirror of your articulated thoughts. To prevent half-formed concepts and mistimed explanations, write out the speech.

5. Plan a lively opening and a forceful closing. When you have completed the five steps, answer this question: "Will my audience know what I hoped they would in Step 1?"

Competent Delivery

More important than the words you choose to say is how you say them. Eloquent prose can go unheard, and mediocre prose can be inspiring and eagerly heard depending on the delivery. Competent delivery entails a performance; many of the skills required for a competent delivery are those of the performer. Practicing your delivery is the key to a fine presentation, just as rehearsals are the key to a flawless performance. Below is a checklist of the major elements of successful delivery. Check those that you need to pay special attention to, and keep them in mind as you rehearse your presentation. To compensate for any negative delivery habits or characteristics you may have, mark your speech at appropriate places, with "stage directions" to remind yourself to take corrective action. For example, do your presentations lack eye contact? Build into your speech places to pan to the audience: look left, center, and right. Do you tend to speak in monotones? Mark your notes with arrows that tell you to say particular words in a raised or lowered tone or to speed up or slow down particular phrases to vary the pace.

Checklist

1. Appearance
   — Wear businesslike (undistracting), comfortable clothes.
   — Maintain a stable stance.
   — Avoid fidgeting (jangling change in the pocket; clicking a ballpoint pen).

2. Voice
   — Vary the pitch, but keep it in lower range.
   — Check for loudness (most people need to talk louder than usual).
   — Check for speed (most people need to talk slower than usual).
   — Enunciate clearly; exaggerate words that you tend to slur.
   — Inject enthusiasm into your tone.

3. Choice of words
   — Use action verbs, and image-conjuring adjectives and nouns.
   — Eliminate or define jargon.

4. Pace
   — Start aggressively, challengingly.
   — Pause or vary loudness and speed for emphasis.
   — Vary the length of sentences in a paragraph.
   — Intersperse visuals, discussion, and hands-on demonstration throughout the lecture.
   — Interject personal asides and anecdotes.

5. Rapport with the audience
   — Make good eye contact.

— Build in participatory activity.
— Encourage (leave time for) discussion.
— Know when to cut off discussion.
— Practice supportive (versus argumentative) responses to skeptical questions.

PROGRAM EVALUATION

Evaluation is the process planners use to find out whether a program or activity is meeting stated objectives and if modifications are necessary to ensure that the desired outcomes are obtained. Evaluation provides information about the current situation and about the degree of success achieved thus far. This kind of information is vital to continued success because it forms the basis for further planning and timely decision making. In other words, evaluation works hand-in-hand with planning to ensure a continuous flow of the knowledge required for assessment, further action, and accountability.

How Can Evaluation Help the Staff-Development Program?

The integration of evaluation into staff-development programs and activities can:

Provide factual information for better decisions, accurate recording of accomplishments, and further planning

Ascertain the relative costs and benefits of a program

Reinforce learning and personal growth

Assess the extent to which objectives are being accomplished

Determine which factors have an impact on staff development

Assure quality control

Document learning experiences

Defend the institution's investment in staff development and justify projected programs

How Can We Get the Most Out of Evaluation?

A Checklist of Questions to Ask Yourself

— How much importance do we place on the evaluation process? Is it an integral part of the staff-development program, or merely something that we will "get around to if time permits?"

— Do we understand the purpose and importance of evaluation? Do we know what we need to evaluate?

— To what extent does our evaluation process lead to long-term planning for staff development? Does our program consist of a series of unrelated "events," with little opportunity for implementing suggested improvements? If so, is there really a need to evaluate? On the other hand, will evaluation have a real impact on our staff-development program planning? Will there be an opportunity to use the information gathered in evaluation to improve what we have done and to plan for the future? If so, do we know what we will do with the information in the short-term and in the long-term?

— What assurances do we have that our evaluation process will yield candid information? Are we committed to openness and honesty in the evaluation process?

— Are we prepared to respond to negative evaluations? Are we ready to implement suggested improvements in content, format, or style? Are we prepared to meet expressed needs for further staff-development activities or topics? Will participants' suggestions be given serious consideration? Will evaluation information be reflected in the planning and presentation of future staff-development activities?

— Do we know how to conduct a valid and useful evaluation? Do we know how, where, and when to get the data we need for subsequent planning? Is the process feasible? Are we willing to spend the time and effort needed to prepare?

— Have we identified the results we expect from the program and activities? Do we know what impact we want the program to have on individuals as well as on the organization? Do we expect changed behavior as a result of the activity? If so, how, when, and how often will we check up on it?

— Can we determine which conditions contribute to or impede the success of the program in achieving its objectives?

— Can we find out what kinds of staff-development activities are most successful from the participants' point of view? Which topics are the most relevant to job responsibilities? Which methods are most effective and worthwhile?

— Is our purpose for evaluation clear? Are we evaluating the impact of the program on the organization? On employees' job performances? Are we evaluating the effectiveness of specific activities or techniques within the program itself? Have we stated the expected results in terms of our chosen goals and objectives?

— In light of our objectives, who will provide the needed information? Employees? Supervisors? Management? Instructors? Will their privacy be protected? Will the process assess these groups' perceptions of new learning or increased competence? What are the potential rewards for learning?

— Do the evaluations indicate the necessity for a follow-up session on the same topics?

— Does the evaluation process measure content coverage and relevancy? Activity design? Use of resources? What are the results in relation to expectations, needs, and costs?

— Which evaluation techniques will be used? Performance tests? Questionnaires? Interviews? Observation?

— How will results be analyzed? Reported? Disseminated? Used?

What Kinds of Evaluation Information should be Collected?

Some Practical Tips

Keep in mind that your evaluation process must meet the needs of your particular organization.

There are costs involved in evaluating a staff-development program—time, money, materials—and these must be weighed against the anticipated benefits. The cost, however, should never be used as an excuse to avoid evaluation altogether.

Evaluation should not be an afterthought, a last-minute ritual performed by giving participants a makeshift reaction form.

Types of Information to Collect

Demographic information on the participants (e.g., age, sex, type of job, duties)

The current state of participants' knowledge, ability, and attitudes.

These could be measured at the beginning and end of a particular activity to assess growth and progress

The participants' expectations at the beginning of the

program and their perceptions of how well those expectations were met

The participants' plans to apply what they have learned to their own job or life situations

The participants' perceptions of the content of the activity and the methods used (Was the topic adequately covered? Was it relevant to their needs? Were there areas which were particularly strong or weak?)

Did the results justify the time and expense? Were the objectives accomplished?

What about the Evaluation Questionnaire?

Evaluators may use a variety of methods to collect information from participants, including tests, interviews, observations, and questionnaires. The method you choose depends on a number of factors. The evaluation questionnaire is the method most people are familiar with, and the one that they are most likely to use. Reasons for selecting this method range from lack of expertise in testing to lack of time for in-depth interviews or follow-up observations. The less familiar methods, however, can produce a wealth of useful information if the evaluator can spend a little extra time learning how to apply them.

The questionnaire itself can be made more useful if the evaluator keeps these few ideas in mind:

Ask thoughtful questions, designed to get the information you are seeking. Do not just ask "yes or no" questions.

Do not ask the participants "how they felt" about the activity. You want to measure the effectiveness of the program, not the participants' current emotional state.

Do not use a questionnaire only at the end of the activity. Try using shorter questionnaires interspersed throughout the program to measure the participants' grasp of the content or to reinforce what they have just learned.

Test your questionnaires before using them to be sure that they are interpreted the way you want them to be interpreted.

Administer follow-up questionnaires to the participants at a later date to reinforce their learning and to find out if they have been able to transfer their learning experience to their own job or life situations.

DEVELOP TRAINING SKILLS

Benefits of Developing Training Skills

Many librarians who are expected to perform training and staff-development functions have little or no formal instruction in teaching methods. Some librarians may have received, in the course of their professional education, an introduction to adult-learning concepts, and some institutions have developed conferences, workshops, and manuals on training adult learners. This type of preparation, however, is not widespread.

In addition to increasing the number of people on the staff able to conduct formal staff-development activities, developing the training skills of librarians has a number of benefits. For example, staff with public-service responsibilities can apply the principles of adult education to general-reference services and bibliographic instruction. Another important benefit is improved communication skills.

Selecting Trainers

1. Identify potential trainers through a survey, referral, or interview.
2. While expertise is important when selecting someone to do training, it is not the only criterion. Characteristics of good trainers include:

Concern for learners

Ability to relate theory to practice

Self-confidence

Openness to different approaches

Ability to listen

Ability to instill confidence in learners

Ability to avoid demeaning or punitive action

Ability to establish a supportive climate

3. Select employees who feel comfortable "on stage" and enjoy making presentations. (One organization has had success in selecting trainers with drama backgrounds.)

Methods of Developing Training Skills

1. Bring in an **outside expert** to train staff, or conduct a workshop in-house if you have someone on staff who knows how to instruct trainers.
2. If your library already has one individual, such as a personnel librarian, who is responsible primarily for coordinating training, send him or her to a conference or institute for special instruction in training skills.
3. Take full advantage of the numerous seminars available on training, facilitation, and presentation skills. The Training Skills Institute sponsored by the Association of Research Library's Office of Management Studies is one such program geared specifically toward libraries.
4. Written manuals and videos on planning and conducting workshops, improving on-the-job training skills, speaking effectively, and a wide variety of other training-related topics are available. These materials can help new trainers develop their

teaching and planning skills.

5. Videotaping practice presentations can be an effective training method. When participants see their own performances, they are less likely to reject criticism and more likely to make appropriate improvements. Group critiques must be carefully solicited, however, so that participants' confidence is enhanced and not weakened.

6. A workshop on training skills should include the following concepts:

   Adult-learning theory. Adult learners, especially those who have not taken classes for several years, need support from their trainers.

   Leadership skills. Success in training ultimately depends on the trainer's ability to encourage learner participation and to guide meaningful group discussions.

   Training design. Trainers should be able to select methods that are suited to particular training needs.

   Administration and logistics. Trainers should know how to select participants, determine the most appropriate schedule, and make effective use of visual aids.

   Practice sessions. Participants should be able to practice new skills before an audience.

   Evaluation and follow-up. The ability to determine the effectiveness of training programs is a critical but often overlooked skill.

7. Trainers-in-training learn by example and by doing. By attending workshops and seminars, they have an opportunity to observe other trainers and to improve their technique. Their first presentations should be carefully reviewed and evaluated by more experienced

trainers.

8. Trainers need recognition from their managers as well as from participants in the program. Their efforts can be recognized in organization newsletters and should be considered during performance evaluations and merit-pay determinations.

TRANSFER OF TRAINING

Transfer of training refers to the individual's ability to apply new procedures or behaviors learned in the classroom to the workplace. Successful transfer involves the acquisition, application, and retention of new skills. Most professionals in the field of human-resource development (HRD) would agree that training is worthwhile only if successful transfer occurs. Un terms of cost-benefit ratios, it makes little sense to invest the time and expense of training and staff-development programs if no measurable improvements in job performance and satisfaction result. However, most HRD professionals would also agree that the incidence of successful transfer is alarmingly low. Recent estimates indicate that more than $100 billion dollars and 15 billion work hours are spent annually on training programs but that as little as 10 percent of the expenditures result in long-term behavior change (Wexley and Baldwin 1986, 503).

The recent interest in transfer-of-training issues may be a result of a precarious economy, slumping productivity, and rapid technological advances requiring new skills and expertise. As the nature of our work becomes more complex and demanding, the need for highly skilled employees becomes increasingly critical. Many libraries have responded to these needs by instituting a series of training and staff-development, programs. Unfortunately, our efforts do not always produce the desired changes. At best, only 40 percent of any training program's content will transfer immediately. After one year, noticeable application of new skills is likely to drop by another 25 percent (Newstrom 1986, 34).

Barriers to Transfer of Training

Why do many training programs fail to produce the desired results? There are a number of plausible explanations for this phenomenon. We sometimes fail to see training programs as a means to an end. We make the mistake of assuming that if we are taught how to do something, we can and will do it. A training program is doomed if we fail to recognize its vulnerability. Therefore, the first and most important step toward improving transfer of training is to admit that it is not automatic.

There are both psychological and organizational barriers to transfer. Frequently, participants either lack confidence in their ability to successfully use the new skills on the job or feel that the values being taught are contrary to existing organizational values. Managers may take a passive attitude toward change and fail to reinforce and reward new behavior. They may not know enough about the skills being taught to identify appropriate changes in job performance. Managers may also fail to reach a mutual understanding with participants as to the desired outcomes (Trost 1985, 79).

Transfer can be defeated during the training session. Many programs fail to break down complex skills into component parts. For example, conflict management requires several basic skills, including the ability to listen, analyze, and handle stressful situations.

If the program is too general, the participants will have difficulty knowing how and when to use specific behaviors. New skills can also fail to transfer if there is insufficient time allowed for classroom practice.

Training and staff-development programs often fail to produce results because there is no follow-up to ensure long-term maintenance of behavior. New skills require a trial-and-error process. Trainees who are unprepared to cope with mistakes may become discouraged and abandon the new approach when desired results are not immediately evident.

What approaches can be taken to overcome these barriers to transfer? Although most attention has focused on the design and content of the training sessions, successful transfer of skills requires that certain actions be taken before, during, and after the training program.

Ensuring Positive Transfer of Training

Program Preparation

Some studies have indicated that even when all the prerequisite motor and cognitive skills are present, performance will be poor if motivation is absent (Noe 1986, 737). Motivation is greater, and transfer of training more likely to occur, if the program is closely matched to the participants' needs. Too often, employees are asked to attend a generic training session that may have little relevance to their jobs. When employees are required to attend a workshop and the reasons are unclear, there may be a lack of motivation or even active resistance to learning.

Participants should be informed of the program's objectives. If they have realistic expectations and know why they have been selected to participate, the program will be more successful. Some advance work, such as introductory reading or self-assessment surveys, will help to prepare the trainees. A pretraining contract can be issued by the trainer specifying what new skills will be learned and what benefits will result if these skills are used on the job.

The work environment must also be examined to determine barriers that may impede transfer. For example, a library wants to do a program on effective reference-question negotiation. The required skills take time to acquire, but the trainer discovers that the reference desk is understaffed and that the librarians feel pressured to answer questions quickly.

In this case, environmental conditions will make it difficult for participants to apply the skills taught in the training program. Although empirical evidence is scant, many HRD professionals believe that *organizational* climate is the most prevalent factor affecting transfer (Newstrom 1986, 37). If significant environmental barriers exist, that particular training program should probably be canceled.

The extent of management support has a major influence on the results of a training program. A lack of support is a common reason why skills learned in the classroom fail to transfer to the workplace. *Without* training is more likely to be perceived as a break from. work and little else. It is crucial that trainers understand the role that managers play in the transfer process and involve them in the planning and preparation stages.

Finally, the participants' initial perceptions of the trainer and the content of the course will affect the degree of transfer. If the trainer is not a credible expert, or if the content of the course is viewed with some skepticism, transfer of training will be minimal (Noe 1986, 742).

Program Implementation

Transfer will depend upon the structure and content of the training program. One common error is to include too much in the program rather than focusing on one of two select skills. A series of short programs ordered in logical progression is often more effective than a single marathon session. If more than one skill is being taught in a single session, negative transfer can occur if the second skill is introduced before the first is mastered (Kelley, Orgel, and Baer 1985, 79-80).

The training program should include theory as well as practical instruction. The principles must be illustrated with appropriate examples that are identical to those occurring in the job environment. If the examples are foreign to the participants, they may reject the principles, and future skill application is unlikely (Leifer and Newstrom 1980, 43). The training program must also give participants an opportunity to practice new skills in the classroom. Hands-on instruction helps participants understand when and how to use new skills. It is less difficult to ensure the transfer of technical and motor skills than behavioral skills. With motor skills, applicable situations are easily identified, and the desired results are virtually guaranteed (Leifer and Newstrom 1980, 42). Most librarians know that it is easier to teach a new circulation clerk how to check out a book than to deal effectively with an angry patron. For this reason, trainers should put special emphasis on the applicability of behavioral and cognitive skills, such as the ability to detect, understand, and remedy a morale problem. If a new skill is applied at the wrong time, the lack of positive results may discourage further effort.

While procedural tasks may be easier to teach, they can still be forgotten after a period of time unless adequate practice occurs during the training session. In one study on procedural tasks described by Joel D. Schendel and Joseph D. Hagman (1982), participants were divided into three groups. One group received overtraining, i.e., repeated practice beyond the first successful performance of a skill. Participants in this group performed better several weeks after the training session than participants who did not practice or practiced only briefly. This and other studies on the effects of overtraining suggest that it is a worthwhile approach to enhance the transfer process.

Trainers should also encourage participants to discuss their experience and observations following practice sessions. Some theorists have argued that the advent of instructional technology, systems learning, and individualized self-paced instruction have interfered with successful transfer because the emphasis is on *atomized* rather than context learning, Many hi-tech instructional packages do not include the opportunity for participants to continuously share what they are learning with others in the program. This opportunity for social transmission during the training process may increase the likelihood of transfer (Ehrenberg 1983, 83).

Maintenance of Behavior

Employees may be motivated to learn new skills, but it, requires much greater motivation to alter their behavior. Employees must be able and willing not only to bring their newly learned skills back to the workplace but to apply those skills over a prolonged period until they become routine.

Even when employees are initially enthusiastic about applying new skills, a number of *inherent* forces usually prevent them from doing so. The most significant factors impeding transfer are related to the organizational climate. They include a lack of on-the-job-reinforcement of new skills, a lack of necessary resources, an absence of managerial interest, and the power of the status *quo*. Higher-level skills that involve interaction with others are especially *vulnerable* to social *deterrents*. Co-workers who did not take the training may be suspicious of any new behavior and react negatively. New supervisory skills can be difficult to apply, particularly when they are different from those used by upper-level management. (We tend to supervise as we are supervised, not as we are taught to supervise) (Mosel 1957, 62).

In addition to the organizational climate, the *employee's abilities* and *attitudes* will affect the degree of transfer. Trainees will be motivated to transfer new skills if they have mastered the content and are aware of the appropriate circumstances in which to apply the new skills. They must perceive that job-performance improvement will likely result, and they must believe that these new skills will be helpful in solving work problems.

A trainee's motivation may be influenced by his or her degree of job involvement. Individuals who are deeply involved in their work are more likely to apply new skills, because improved job performance is a significant source of self-esteem (Noe 1986, 742-43). A trainee's "locus-of-control" will also have an effect on the motivation to learn and apply new skills. Those with an internal locus-of-control believe that job performance is contingent on their own behavior and is, therefore, within their control. For this reason, these individuals may *exert* greater effort in collecting information and attempting new procedures (Noe 1986, 739).

Training is a process, not an episode. To make sure that skills successfully transfer may require a series of meetings between trainer and trainee. Follow-up sessions should be designed to help participants refine their skills and to encourage continued practice. Participants should have a plan specifying when and how they intend to use their new skills. They should be prepared to document the results in a *progress report,* which can be forwarded to the supervisor. Discussion groups can be set up within the organization to help reinforce new behavior.

For training programs to be cost-effective, management support and interest in the program must continue throughout the process. Without positive recognition from the supervisor, the benefits associated with change may appear uncertain, and it may be difficult for the individual to see sufficient *intrinsic* reward to sustain the new behavior.

While external sources of positive feedback are important, some experts claim that skill retention is largely a self-managed effort (Marx 1986, 55). Any new behavior is *susceptible* to *relapse,* and trainees must be aware of this tendency and learn to cope with it. Current relapse-prevention theory is derived from research on addicts that has shown the unfortunate consequences of a single lapse in behavior. Relapse prevention emphasizes gradual improvement.

If employees expect to see immediate results, then slow progress may convince them that they are unable to make the changes (Marx 1982,438). Without *relapse-prevention training*, a temporary lapse may be seen as a total failure. The employee may attribute this failure to personal inadequacy rather than lack of skills, and the old, less-effective routines will seem preferable (Marx 1982, 436). Relapse-prevention training focuses on the identification of high-risk situations. For example, a circulation clerk attends a training session on dealing calmly with angry patrons. She is able to practice her new skills successfully when she feels confident. She should be aware, however, that certain high-risk situations, such as criticism from her supervisor, may make her overly sensitive to a patron's complaints.

Goal setting is another important post-training strategy designed to maintain behavior. Goals, especially those that are made publicly, will increase the trainee's commitment to making the necessary changes. Self-managed techniques, such as goal setting and relapse prevention, are important to include in any training program because external sources of reinforcement may be absent or unpredictable.

TRAINING PLACE

Library administrators, managers, and trainers need to work together to ensure that staff-development programs include strategies that facilitate change. Training programs which encourage flexibility and adaptation are as critical as supervisory training. Librarians must learn to manage change as effectively as they manage people.

The process of change has been the subject of much discussion and research in the last twenty years. This research has revealed that certain strategies for planning and implementing change are more successful than others. Successful strategies include involving staff in the planning process, targeting opinion leaders, and informing staff of desired and undesired outcomes (Fine 1986). Training programs which apply these strategies are more likely to produce well-trained staff who support and actively use a new technology or procedure. Without incorporating these strategies into training programs, libraries will be less able to cope with the new demands and developments that are transforming our work.

Training for Change

Understanding why staff accept change is an essential component of the training process. Research on the process of change can tell us which characteristics of individuals, ideas, and organizations lead to accommodation of change and to innovation and which factors produce resistance. For example, Everett M. Rogers (1983, 258) indicates that individuals with well-developed interpersonal communication skills are more likely to adopt innovation. Individuals who are fearful of the negative consequences of change will certainly be more resistant.

In her study on change-agent characteristics of library professionals, Jo Anne A. Hall (1984) concludes that libraries should supply information on the change process in their staff-development programs and help librarians identify and assume the roles of change agents. According to Hall's recommendations, a staff-development officer can stimulate change by developing programs which teach personal networking skills and which include some role-playing sessions on change a gentry. Staff who are aware of their own potential to effect change and who are familiar with strategies for winning acceptance for new ideas and procedures will be able to play an active role in the process of change.

Other research on the process of change indicates that a new idea will have a greater chance of being accepted if it is easily adapted, compatible with existing procedures, and has a demonstrable advantage over other, solutions (Rogers 1983, 213-31). Training sessions should stress these factors. For example, a typical training program for a new automated circulation system might include the following procedures: charge, discharge, renewal, fines, and holds. A change-oriented agenda would cover the same general procedures but might begin with a presentation on the advantages of automation and conclude with a *brainstorming* session on adapting existing processes to the new technology.

Rogers also observes that innovative change can sometimes begin with the awareness of a solution, which is then matched with an existing organizational problem (Rogers 1983, 213-31). Rogers calls this phenomenon "scanning for innovation." Adaptive and flexible organizations are regularly scanning the environment for creative and new approaches and ideas. A change-oriented staff-development program should encourage employees to scan for innovation. Routing current journals, fostering attendance at professional meetings, providing access to electronic mail and other discussion forums, and planning brainstorming sessions after conferences are some of the ways in which staff-development personnel can coordinate innovation scanning and problem solving in the library.

Staff-development officers play an important role in promoting organizational growth and development by promoting change in their training programs. They can help staff understand and become more comfortable with the change process by emphasizing the advantages of change to the organization as well as the individual. They can also help staff to take a direct part in creating change by encouraging them to look for new ideas, approaches, and services in the literature and in discussions with colleagues. These strategies are just a few examples of how positive change can be the focus of training sessions.

Role Modeling and Change Agentry

Adequate raining is one way to enhance an employee's talent and ability to cope with rapid change. However, a welcoming climate and individuals who initiate and promote change are necessary as well. Thomas W. Shaughnessy (1988) and others share the opinion that organizational climate in libraries may have a greater effect on proposed change than some managers might think. Organizational climate is controlled by many factors, including the library's staff-development program. New employees develop their sense of the library based on interaction with others and on orientation sessions. The focus of introductory training, as well as the emphasis placed on staff development, typifies what is important in a particular library. The structure of the staff-development programs is a signpost to new employees advising them of the possible rewards and penalties associated with innovative behavior. In addition, it is particularly important that staff-development officers and trainers practice the change strategies they preach. Trainers and staff developers themselves should be comfortable with change and should regularly place themselves in the role of change agent. They should be "movers and shakers" or, at very least, be able to recognize and encourage the "movers and shakers" in their library.

What distinguishes a change-receptive staff-development program from a more traditional staff-development effort? Charles R. Martell (1983, 63) suggests that staff development in a dynamic environment should include "elements of autonomy, self-regulation and *discretionary* decision making." Literature on the process of change uniformly supports staff participation in decision making to help encourage a widespread sense of ownership and commitment. A change-structured staff-development program should emphasize self-directed performance goals explicitly related to change priorities. As an employee progresses, development personnel should shift from being a program trainer to a facilitator, providing resources for self-directed learning.

How do these theories and strategies relate to the creation of a new presentation or workshop? The theory of change suggests that staff should be part of deciding what the program topic should be. Staff should also take part in investigating alternative opportunities for obtaining the same information. In addition, the theory of successful change suggests that programs might best be created by employees with the assistance of staff developers, rather than the other way around. Increasing staff responsibility for their own professional development and rewarding staff for implementing innovative concepts are important components of a change-oriented staff-development program.

What does a change agent do and how can a trainer be an agent of change? In defining some of the roles of a change agent, Ronald G. Havelock (1973) stresses that a change agent works to establish a healthy relationship with employees in which expectations are realistic, both parties are willing to negotiate and compromise when necessary, and communication is adequate and open. As a catalyst for change, the trainer works toward promoting a common purpose, is sensitive to opportunities for change, and implements new procedures when staff seem most receptive to change. For example, there are at least two ways to train staff on a new software package. The trainer can simply present a step-by-step rundown of the procedures and the basic mechanics.

However, a trainer who wants to ensure that staff will use the new software might solicit testimonials from other librarians, determine which department would benefit the most and train them first, and schedule the training session when there are *apt* to be few *disruptions* and distractions. In other words, the staff developer becomes more than a trainer—the staff developer becomes a promoter or a catalyst for change.

Another role mentioned by Havelock is that of the resource linker. A trainer acting as a resource linker assists employees in their pursuit of additional knowledge. In this example, the trainer may provide the names of software experts, identify relevant reading materials, and help the employee to build personal networks inside and outside the library.

ASSESSING TRAINING NEEDS

A useful starting point in assessing training needs could be to review the service itself to establish its main thrust and to see what changes need to be made, for example, in providing current awareness services, or setting up a business information service. These would certainly require in the first case a keen awareness of the employing organization's constantly changing activities and its plans for the future, as well as communication skills and the ability to select the most appropriate medium for its delivery, e.g. disseminating information in hard-copy form as a printed bulletin or via electronic mail, according to the norms and procedures which seem to operate most successfully in responding to organizational needs. In the second case, that of setting up a business information service, an understanding of the business environment, its language and how it operates, plus the ability to work to tight deadlines and retain the enquirer's confidence would be essential.

As the case study suggests, in assessing training needs there will be across-the-board organizational considerations and more specific departmental requirements. In considering the organization as a whole, one might start by asking such questions as:

- Is there a central training function?
- What is the overall policy towards training?
- Is there a career structure in place?
- Are there any internal guidelines for managers to follow, for example in conducting appraisals as part of the development process or in evaluating training?
- Is there an organizational staff manual setting out, among other things, training and development practices and procedures?
- What has the organization already promised the individual in the letter of offer?

- What expectations were set at the interview stage?

On a departmental basis the following types of question would need to be asked:

- What has already taken place, perhaps on an ad hoc basis, within the department?
- Are you able to support the requirements of the library/information professional associations in terms of either the qualification process, or continuing professional development?
- How do these fit into the organizational framework?

The way in which such questions were addressed by a Scottish public library service provides an excellent model, as set outlates in this chapters.

THREE PERSPECTIVES

For any existing training need or deficiency, three perspectives can be considered: the individual perspective (that of the trainer or trainee), the perspective of the operational unit, and the perspective of the library as a whole. Each typically relates to the perceived benefits or losses associated with a particular solution. Benefits and losses can affect the individual, the unit, and the entire organization (Datta 1978). Training involves change, and change often represents a combination of gains and losses, although a gain for one individual or operational unit does not necessarily mean a gain for another.

The trainer who conducts a needs assessment should examine each possible perspective for two reasons. First, it is important to determine the perspective or view of the problem that is most appropriate for the situation. Second, the trainer must confirm that training is the most effective means of resolving the problem. These two requirements may appear obvious to the reader, but they can be easily overlooked when staff-development plans are being discussed. It is important to remember that not every performance problem can be solved through additional training and staff development.

During the needs-assessment process, the perspective provided by the individual is often related to personal concerns, such as lack of job satisfaction or frustration over *ambiguous* performance evaluations. A needs assessment which considers the individual perspective might uncover problems such as burnout and fatigue among several employees. The appropriate solutions in this case may focus on adjusted work loads or additional staff rather than on new training programs.

The perspective of the operational unit will be focused primarily on maximum efficiency and will be less concerned with individual needs. This broader perspective often addresses critical issues that individual members within the operational unit might ignore. The needs assessment which takes this perspective might generate solutions that address, for example, inadequate skill levels or a lack of motivation among staff members.

The needs assessment which takes the library's perspective will be the broadest in scope. It might focus on budgetary concerns, comprehensive staff-development programs, and deficiencies that are widespread among operational units. Solutions based on this perspective might reflect the general goals of the parent institution—such as the goals of a university administration.

Models of Needs Assessments

In addition to examining needs from different perspectives, the trainer may adopt several other assessment approaches. Floyd C. Pennington (1980) identified *six clusters of needs-assessment models*, which vary in scope, purpose, and effectiveness.

1. *System-Discrepancy Model.* This is the most common needs-assessment approach. It attempts to measure the difference between the current situation and some optimum level of performance and service by analyzing the gap between actual skills or knowledge and desired skills or knowledge. The problems with this approach stem from the difficulty of defining precisely what the optimum situation should be (Scriven and Roth 1978).

2. *Self-fulfillment.* This is a market-strategy approach that targets the interests or wants of a specified group and then presents training opportunities that cater to those interests. Despite its label, one weakness of this approach is that it ignores individual learning needs and skill development and addresses only common preferences.

3. *Individual Appraisal.* Unlike the self-fulfillment model, this approach encourages the individual to determine his or her own learning needs. Its major weakness is the difficulty that many people have in honestly assessing their own weaknesses and inabilities.

4. *Diagnostic.* This approach defines a need as a harmful deficiency or organizational illness. It discusses needs assessment in terms of general-performance deficits and treatments. A weakness of this model is the difficulty that many organizations have in translating broad prescriptions into feasible actions.

5. *Analytic.* This model focuses upon linear problem solving and continued improvement rather than on a onetime remediation. It may be difficult to apply because of the level of *abstraction* and advanced problem-solving skill required to outline a complex series of actions.

6. *Democratic.* This model stresses interactional group efforts in the determination of needs. Unfortunately, the need to reach a consensus may result in an *imprecise* analysis of critical issues, and the process can be very time consuming.

Regardless of the needs-assessment model selected, the perspective will determine how the problem is defined and what, if any, training programs are employed. Although the models vary in scope and method, the needs-assessment process will include a few basic components which apply to all models.

Components of a Needs Assessment

Judith Fidler and David R. Loughran (1980) define three major steps in the needs-assessment process: a thorough identification of the problem, a classification of the probable causes of the problem, and the generation of possible solutions. The system-discrepancy model can be used to illustrate these steps.

The first step involves identifying and describing specific, observable performances and comparing the existing situation with some operational standard. For example, existing *interlibrary* loan (ILL) statistics can be compared with an operational standard. This standard might specify that a certain number of ILL requests are reviewed and processed in one hour at 95 percent accuracy.

The second step involves classifying the causes of any discrepancy between the present level of performance and the intended goal. A performance discrepancy can be caused by lack of skills, an environmental disturbance, or insufficient employee motivation and incentive. By classifying the problem, those discrepancies that can be solved through training can be readily identified. The purpose of this phase is to ensure that training efforts are not wasted on problems that require a different approach.

The third step in needs assessment, according to Fidler and Loughran, is the generation of possible solutions based on the information gathered in the first two steps and the selection of the one that is most cost-beneficial. Making this step the final phase of the planning process will guard against our natural tendency to determine solutions before the problem is fully understood. A prepackaged training program or workshop may sound appealing to the personnel librarian or staff-development officer, but much of the effort and cost needed to provide this training will be wasted if the solution does not fulfill a predetermined need. The tendency to be solution or action oriented can result in the "ready-fire-aim" syndrome, which rarely produces the desired outcomes (Hobbs 1990).

CASE STUDY : GLASGOW CITY LIBRARIES - I

Introduction : It is Council policy that each Department will produce an annual Training Plan and that this shall be submitted to the Director of Personnel for approval. The following 'Notes for Guidance' have been compiled to assist Heads of Department and those responsible for coordinating departmental training and development requirements who may wish to adopt a more structured approach to the planning and forecasting of training and development activities within their departments.

Benefits of a Training Plan

The formulation of a Training Plan should result in the following benefits.

(i) The training and development needs of employees are identified and catered for in a structured manner, through a systematic analysis of what is required. Factors which would be considered in carrying out such an analysis would include:

- current and future job requirements

- maintaining or improving the performance of employees within their jobs
- employees with potential
- any special needs of groups or individual employees, arising from, for example, technological change, reorganization or the introduction of new procedures within the department
- needs arising from the Council's Staff Assessment and Development Scheme.

(ii) The training and development needs of employees are seen as an integral part of the department's short and medium term aims and objectives, thereby ensuring the training and development of employees makes a positive contribution to departmental activities.

(iii) The persons responsible for the training and development of employees within a department are clearly identified and levels of accountability defined.

(iv) A record is provided of the training and development activities carried out by a department as a whole, creating the basis for reviewing the effectiveness of training and allocating future resources.

(v) It demonstrates an active commitment to the training and development of employees within a department in line with the Council's overall 'Training Policy'.

Conducting the Analysis

Generally speaking training and development needs may arise either from key strategic or operational issues facing the Department or from individual job needs. Gathering the information on what is required for the coming year can be carried out by a variety of methods. These range from detailed interviews with departmental managers responsible for employees and their development, to a simple memo or questionnaire asking those concerned to outline their requirements for the year ahead in line with departmental objectives.

The method chosen therefore, is left entirely to the departmental management involved in collecting the data and will obviously depend on the resources available. However an important source of information on individual needs will be the Employee Assessment and Development Scheme.

Structuring the Training Plan

To assist the person responsible for formulating the Training Plan an outline structure is attached. This model Training Plan is divided into six sections:

1. Strategic aims of the Department
2. Major operational issues facing the Department
3. Training and Development priorities
4. Departmental Personnel Summary
5. Training Budget
6. Training and Development Action Plan

This, it should be emphasised, is not the only format that is acceptable but represents good practice in basing employee development on the real needs of the Department as well as on each individual's natural desire for personal and career development.

> *Nevertheless, in determining whether a Department's training and development plan is acceptable the Director of Personnel will as a minimum standard require the information referred to in sections 4, 5 and 6 of the model plan.* That is:

- The Departmental Personnel Summary
- The Departmental Training Budget (analysed as appropriate)
- The Training and Development Action Plan.

The Action Plan is intended to encompass only *off-the-job* training and development activities. The development of staff through work activities (special projects, job rotation, coaching by their Manager *etc.*) should be planned and managed through the Employee Assessment and Development Scheme.

The Director of Libraries recognises the Council's Policy for the training and development of its staff which states:

> "The Council recognises that training has an important contribution to make in the achievement of its corporate objectives and in the maintenance of an effective, well motivated workforce. The Council is therefore prepared to make available appropriate training facilities which will enable employees to acquire the aptitude, skills, knowledge and qualifications necessary to perform effectively the duties and responsibilities of their posts. The training provided will also take account of the needs of employees to develop their potential for future employment at more senior levels".

This plan sets out the Libraries Department's approach to the implementation of the Council's training and development policy objectives which are as follows;

1. to ensure that the Council has sufficient trained, qualified and experienced employees to meet its service needs and to ensure its continuing effectiveness in providing services;
2. to provide the training needed to enable employees to perform their present jobs more effectively and to

acquire the necessary new skills when they move into new or different areas of work;

3. to assist employees to develop their potential and to realise their aspirations for career progression consistent with the needs of both the Council and individual employees;
4. to ensure that there is equality of opportunity for employees to obtain systematic training;
5. to meet the training and development needs of employees in the most effective way, in terms of quality and cost, by using the Council's own resources or, where this is not appropriate, by the utilisation of external training facilities and services.

The Plan is split into six sections:

1. Strategic Aims of the Department
2. Major operational issues facing the Department
3. Training and development priorities
4. Departmental Personnel Summary
5. Training Budget
6. Training and Development Action Plan (for off-the-job activities)

This document therefore constitutes the Libraries Department's record of intent regarding the training and development of its employees in line with the departmental objectives and plans for the year 1991/1992.

The Plan takes account of the training and development needs of all employees within the department arising from:

- council policies including commitments arising from the manifesto of the majority political group;
- current and future job requirements;

- the need to improve or maintain the performance of employees within their jobs;
- developing employees with potential;
- any special needs of groups or individual employees resulting from technological change, reorganisation or the introduction of new procedures within the department;
- needs arising from the Council's Employee Assessment and Development Scheme.

Strategic Aims of the Department

Training and development of staff is an important investment in supporting fulfilment of key departmental aims. The key aims of your department should be listed here.

They may be derived from such sources as the manifesto of the majority political group, from Council and Committee decisions, from internal strategy documents or from the annual budget process.

List Key Aims

Glasgow City Libraries as a Department of Glasgow City Council has three strategic aims:

1. in lending services to provide library material in all forms for home use by the public, community information and enquiry services from a network of libraries;
2. in reference services to maintain by acquisition and presentation a comprehensive collection of books and other material for reference and study; provide from that material and through computer databases a wide ranging reference and public information service; and

3. in administrative services to control and manage the department and provide support services for all departments.

(II)

Major Operational Issues

At a more detailed level training and development needs for groups of staff and individuals can arise from policy and procedural changes, new legislation, new technology, new working methods as a result of the demands of competitive tendering or a range of other specific factors. The implications of such changes may be reflected in the outcomes of Employee Assessment and Development interviews.

This section should focus only on the main issues seen as having important training and development implications for the department.

List Main Issues

1. The implementation of changes in work practice arising from the MSU report on lending and reference services.
2. Extend the use of the automated issue system to include fines for overdue material and variable loan periods.
3. Continue with the introduction of CD-ROMs to replace or augment hard copy.
4. Increase the use of libraries by 5%.
5. Reduce departmental absenteeism.

(III)

Training and Development Priorities

Having outlined the main challenges facing the Department in the previous two sections, this section should be used to highlight the main skills, knowledge and attitudes that will have to be acquired by employees as a result. What training needs are implied in the strategy and in the operational issues? What has emerged from Employee Assessment and Development? Another source of information on training needs will be the person specification drawn up prior to recruiting new members of staff. Where possible, reference should be made to the main employee groupings for whom a particular training and development response is appropriate.

List Training & Development Priorities

1. As a result of the Management Services review, four new posts of Heads of Division have been created. These posts carry considerably greater responsibility for budget allocation and the monitoring and control of expenditure within a division of approximately ten service points. The new post-holders will almost certainly require training in budgeting and financial control, the departmental budgeting system and in adapting to change.

2. Manual workers will be included in a greater variety of courses in the coming years. It is this department's intention to train all manual workers in Customer Care and Sensory Awareness. We also intend to introduce an updated general safety course as well as a Supervisory Skills programme for Shift Leaders. Drivers will undergo HGV training in order to comply with EEC regulations.

3. Training in Employee Assessment and Development will continue to include grades AP2 down to GS1. All employees will attend the two day in-house course.

4. Induction training (half-day) for all new entrants will take place within the first month of commencing employment and library assistants will receive additional training.

5. All Mitchell Library Staff will attend a new course, "Sensory Awareness", to enable them to cope better with customers with sensory disabilities. Customer Care for library assistants will be introduced this year (especially for new entrants).

6. The Young Peoples Services Department will continue to offer a variety of courses to enable staff to either update or acquire new skills in order that the service can be maintained and improved. For example, courses in Story telling, Book Selection, School Visits and Merchandising and Display.

7. Discipline, Grievance and Counselling—it is intended that all designated supervisors attend this course to enable them to deal with changes in the Council's Absence Monitoring Scheme as well as enhancing their managerial skills,

8. The First Line—the supervisory development programme will be run in-house for the first time this year and focus on the particular needs of the department's supervisors.

9. The need for training in Marketing the Service has been highlighted by the EAD Scheme and priority will be placed on seeking appropriate courses to meet individual and departmental needs.

(IV)

Departmental Personnel Summary

This section should set out the actual establishment levels for the main categories of staff in the Department. The way staff are classified may vary slightly from department to department but a common classification might be: Management, Supervisory, Technical, Professional, Administrative/Clerical, Manual. Please be specific in defining each group.

Group & Section	Number
APT&C	
Directorate	4
Administrative services	44
Lending services	
Reference services	101
Total APT & C	500
MANUAL	
Administrative services	44
Lending services	73
Total manual	117
TEMPORARY	10
MATERNITY LEAVE	16

(V)

Departmental training Budget 1990-1991

Total Training Budget £ -----(insert figure)

NB. Please include estimated expenditure on conferences.

Departmental Training Budget Analysis

If appropriate please indicate below the main subheadings within your department's Training Budget (e.g. Further Education, Courses, Continuing Professional Development *etc.*)

(VI)

LIST MAIN BUDGET

The Training and Development Action Plan

On the following pages you should list the off-the-job activities planned to meet the Training and Development priorities identified in Section Three. Account should also be taken of agreed individual training and development activities identified through the Employee Assessment and Development Scheme.

It may be useful to use separate sheets for the various categories of staff identified in Section Four. Some Departments may also wish to separate Further Education provision from other development activities.

Drawing up the Action Plan

Use an A4 sheet of paper (landscape) to draw up your departmental action plan. Head each sheet with the name of the Department and the Staff Group. Please use a separate sheet for each staff group listed in Section Four. Each sheet should be divided into vertical columns with the following headings:

1. Employee Group or Individual
2. Off-the-Job Training and Development Activity Course Title
3. Objectives of the Activity
4. Responsibility
5. Duration (in days)
6. No. of Employees involved
7. Budget (where appropriate) in £

Each column should be completed as follows:

Column 1. should identify as specifically as possible the groups and individuals for whom a particular training and development activity is intended.

Column 2. should specify the nature of the activity. This should include the full range of possible off-the-job training and development opportunities including:

Secondments	Open Learning
Seminars	Further Education
Visits	User Groups
Conferences	

It should also wherever possible include details of the supplier of any training or other service (e.g. Central Personnel Training and Development, College, external trainer *etc.*).

Column 3. should specify as precisely as possible why the training and development activity is being carried out and what it is hoped to achieve. It should be possible after training and development has occurred to say whether the objectives have been achieved.

Column 4. should name the member of staff who will have responsibility for organising each training and development activity and for ensuring it is carried out.

Column 5. provides information on the duration in days of each activity. This will in most cases be best expressed as the number of days away from normal duties (e.g. a one year course of further education will probably involve 30 days away from normal duties if on a day release basis).

Column 6. provides information on the number of employees involved.

Column 7. provides an estimate of the cost of the activity where this is appropriate. This should take into account travel, subsistence and other reimbursements, as we has normal course fees.

As the above case study illustrates, training should not be viewed as something which takes place in isolation from the employing organization, although some of the activities may take place outside that organization. In establishing the training needs of the individual, the manager is also required to be able to justify them in terms of the organization's needs.

STAFF DEVELOPMENT TRAINING : METHODS

There are a number of general work activities such as staff meetings, working parties and committees which can encourage learning and the demonstration of initiative . Even if only one member of staff can take part in these, a feeling of wider involvement can be achieved by feedback from the participant through discussion and the' circulation of papers, subject to any confidentiality procedures which have to be observed. The learning which can take place in these activities is based not only on acquiring subject knowledge or familiarity with technical processes, but offers considerable opportunity to observe meetings behaviour and to learn what makes it successful - the skills of control and negotiation - and to develop an organizational perspective rather than just a departmental one. This is particularly important in the library and information business, where maximum contributions can only be made by gaining this broader understanding.

Attendance at meetings and membership of working parties and committees usually reflects the US department's involvement in, and responsibility for, various central organizational activities, e.g. records management, internal database development and maintenance, certain specialist areas of expertise and knowledge possessed by staff, such as languages, or the specific emphasis of the service, e.g. in regularly monitoring and analysing subject fields related to the organization's pursuit of its objectives.

The training activities used in the Stoy Hayward programme included on-the-job training and attendance at meetings as discussed above, as well as visits to other library and information centres, and internal and external courses. These were supported by regular counselling sessions, guided reading and a personal project. Where the candidate was pursuing the Library Association Route to Associate-ship they were also encouraged to maintain a logbook. This is not only useful as a record from which to start preparation of the required Library Association Professional Development Report for Associateship, it also allows the candidate to monitor and review personal progress. As such it could prove valuable to all trainees, whether or not they are pursuing a professional qualification.

There are a number of useful training techniques and methods, ranging from the formal course involving lectures interspersed with group and individual activities, to task-based training with constant feedback. Some methods will be better suited to certain areas of the programme, e.g. the improvement of presentation skills requires practice and is well suited to the participative approach with use of video or CCTV recording and subsequent analysis of presentations made by individuals to a group. The participative course needs to be in the hands of a skilled and experienced trainer with an understanding of the behavioural considerations, that is, not only of the reaction of others to the presentation itself, but also of the underlying feelings of the person preparing and making the presentation. This, like any other situation in which individuals find themselves highly exposed, has to be handled with extreme sensitivity. Role playing requires similar treatment and any role-playing situation and characters must be carefully thought out in terms of relevance to the participants' needs, with subsequent feedback if its learning objectives are to be met. When either setting up a training course yourself, or considering others which may be available, it could be useful to ask the following initial questions about the training methods/materials which may be employed:

- How will the training be conducted, e.g. on a one-to-one or on a group basis; face-to-face or by remote training; on a 'demonstrate-then-practise' basis; lecture/discussion?
- What range and mix of methods/materials arc available?
- Which would be most appropriate given the stated objectives and the identified audience?
- What training skills are required to maximize the effective use of such materials/methods?

There are a number of commonly used methods/materials as listed below:

- Lecture/presentation
- Demonstration
- Participation
- Discussion
- Group activities
- Role playing
- Simulation exercise
- One-to-one training
- Use of manual tasks
- Question sheets
- Puzzles
- Flipcharts
- Black/white boards
- Overhead projector and transparencies
- Carousel and slides
- Data tablet and computer graphics
- Films, videos
- Audio cassettes
- Compact discs
- Computer packages.

Each training method requires you, as the trainer, to consider how to get the most out of it through practice and preparation, so do test it out, preferably with a colleague acting as the audience. That way you will find out what works, and which alternative methods might be appropriate.

Courses—Internal and External

Short courses are valuable as a training method not only because they give the trainee the opportunity to be immersed in and concentrate on a particular area of new knowledge for a period of time without distraction, but also because of the benefits of interacting with others in the learning process. This applies to both internal and external courses, both of which bring a number of benefits. For example, working on an internal course with people from oilier departments between which there has been little previous contact, can add to each participant's knowledge and understanding of the organization. It is also likely to increase and improve communication across departments, increasing the assistance that each can provide to the other and enhancing work relationships.

External courses provide a forum for the exchange of ideas with others who, although representing a variety of different organizations, nevertheless share common experiences. This can suggest new ways of handling situations and procedures, and solutions to problems. External courses also provide networks of contacts for future reference. The purpose and level of external courses should be clearly stated in the course literature, and are vital to the manager in the process of selecting courses.

If you want to know more about the emphasis of a specific part of the course, or to discuss the appropriateness of the level at which it is pitched, always ring the course providers, who should be able to clarify these points or suggest a more appropriate course for your purpose. It is also useful to talk to those in other organizations who might have used the courses. Seek their perception of the success or suitability of certain training events, which will be based on the feedback from their attendee in conjunction with their own management observation of the outcome of that piece of training. Short courses vary in format and duration. They may be based oil a series of presentations by one or more lecturers, they may include practical work and demonstrations. Their intention could be to introduce new entrants to the LIS profession to the basic skills required; to update experienced LIS workers on various topics; or to provide a means of refreshing those returning to work after a career break.

Visual Aids

When preparing training materials, the trainer needs to consider the most effective way of getting the message across. The underlying key is *keep it simple*, and even the most sophisticated equipment can DC used to present ideas in a clear and uncomplicated way, but as with all training aids and equipment it is the way in which it is used that dictates its success or otherwise.

The simple rule is always to try to see the visual aid as the audience will see it. For example, all lettering displayed, whether on a flipchart or via transparencies or computer graphics, needs to be clear and large enough.

The overhead projector properly used is a valuable training aid. However, a few basic rules can help: switch it off when changing transparencies - a bright patch of light on a blank white screen can be visually very trying for those facing it. Transparencies can be revealed in their entirety or a line at a time as appropriate. Again, switch off in between each point if discussion is to take place before moving on.

Little and often is the way to impart information, so avoid long groups of words. Make use of colour and try to create materials that are visually pleasing. These simple rules apply to all types of visual presentation.

The inclusion of training films and pre-recorded videos should not be regarded as an easy option to keep the delegates happy, or to avoid the preparation of additional material - like other training material, they are available to be used, not just shown. Such training materials, which quite often illustrate good and bad practice, can form the basis of a number of activities.

For example, participants may be asked to observe and make notes of main points for subsequent structured group discussion, which in turn could lead to the group or individuals being required to draw up action plans. Most commercially produced training materials are accompanied by well-designed literature, usually with separate booklets for delegates and course' leaders These frequently include exercises which can be used to bring home the message. Films and videos are often used as case study exercises, placing participants in certain work situations and requiring them to respond by exercising their judgement and coming up with solutions to the problems portrayed.

Group Activities

Not all case studies are film-based: a number of the lengthier ones used in management development provide the participants with sets of documents describing the situation to be resolved. The documents act as the starting point for in-depth group discussion, into which role playing or simulation activities may be incorporated. Such activities also bring to light personal skills, abilities and qualities, for example those of leadership, negotiation or problem solving.

Group activities are not limited to use on courses, they also provide a valuable means of constructive discussion within the department, if properly structured. A regular monthly staff meeting will be more effective if there is a pre-stated key issue or topic of interest to be discussed. Staff need to be encouraged both to prepare their thoughts for this and to contribute these at the meeting. Group discussion can help improve ways of handling certain areas of work. Brainstorming has long been recognized as an effective means of problem solving.

One example of the successful and constructive use of brainstorming is in the area of service review. It is quite common for this to place the emphasis on user opinion - after all, the service is there for the users-but don't forget to seek ideas from staff as well. If you are planning to conduct a user survey, why not conduct a similar one among your staff? Hopefully they will already have been involved in the setting up of the user survey, e.g. in the design of any questionnaire or checklist to be used, so it would be a natural next step for them to put their own ideas into place.

Each member of staff should start by writing down as many ideas as possible, being encouraged to use their imagination and come up with innovative ideas for taking the service forward, which can include changing existing activities, both in terms of the front-end service offered and the underlying procedures which make it possible, as well as replacing old with new. Then the brainstorming begins as each member of staff puts forward ideas which in turn stimulate others. Brainstorming can be an extremely useful means of staff development and, when used as described above, can considerably aid service development as well.

Independent Learning

An increasingly popular and flexible means of offering training and development opportunities is by the use of self-study, often through computer-based learning for specific areas, or through distance learning packages. In the case of some longer courses leading to a particular qualification, they may also provide access to a personal tutor. This will sometimes be on a face-to-face basis, but is often via telephone or written communication. This form of self-driven learning requires considerable commitment and discipline from the trainee, with support and assistance from the manager and the employing organization. Self-study is an appropriate method for both qualification-based courses and other areas of study which make up the process of continuing professional development. The *Best practice* research, cited in earlier chapters, found that although some participants were not always able to get away from the workplace to attend all the courses they would like to, their employers were often willing to purchase self-study material for them, and in some cases to allocate study time for their use. Although such forms of training should not completely replace course attendance, which has many benefits, it does offer opportunities to pursue study which may not otherwise be made available. As with other methods of training there are both advantages and disadvantages: the main advantage is that of flexibility in terms of pacing by the individual to suit their own needs, with the likelihood of strong reinforcement and retention of the learning because of the nature of the process.

The main disadvantage is likely to be a feeling of isolation and lack of direction or awareness of progress without the presence of a mentor, again underlining the importance of feedback in any training situation. Appropriate design of distance learning material is therefore crucial to the learning process. Having decided on the likely audience, along with the results required, the author of the package needs to focus on structure and style, aiming for clarity with brevity. Constant review during the preparation will help identify possible problems the student might encounter, and allow provision to be made for these through the use of appropriate teaching techniques.

Layout and presentation plays a large part in motivating the student and retaining interest. A useful pamphlet on the subject of distance learning for those working in libraries is that produced by Dale in the Library Association's series *Guidelines for training in libraries.* This includes some helpful checklists for those who might be planning to actually prepare training material in a form suitable for distance learning, and a list of organizations who would be able to provide further guidance. Haythornthwaite and White's survey of distance learning packages offered by library schools and other institutions in the English-speaking world will act as a good starting point. Although published in 19S9, it does provide the means for managers to update the list of what is available by contacting any or all of the many institutions referred to.

Presentation of Material

The preparation of any form of training material needs to be carefully thought through, with both the objectives of the training and the needs of the individual in mind. The first step is to establish what appropriate material already exists - there is no point in expending a lot of time and effort, perhaps at the expense of other management activities, in preparing a training package when a suitable one is readily available. Of course you will wish to establish that it is suitable for the particular purpose you have in mind, but it is always worth considering whether it could be adapted to your needs, perhaps in combination with other material. You may find that it presents an aspect of the topic under con- sideration that you had not thought of covering, but which could usefully be included. Your main criteria are likely to be:

- That it covers the subject to the degree of detail required
- That it is presented at the right level
- That it is well presented and interesting.

Today's sophisticated level of presentation by most media sets high expectations - the amateur video or poorly written document will simply not have credibility in the eyes of the recipient and the training message will certainly be lost. Even apparently simple written communications, such as instructions for the use of equipment, need to be clearly expressed and well set out if they are to be effective. It is often the task of a junior member of staff to prepare labels and notices, but if that person is given no guidance it is unlikely that there will be a consistent standard or style.

Yet labels and notices are part of the outward display of the library/information service and as such need to look professional, as well as performing their job of guiding the user. Whether such signs and instructions are good or bad, they will still make an impression, and it is up to you to ensure that these simple but vital tasks are covered by your training programme, bearing in mind that the trainee needs to know why, as well as how.

The standard advice on written communications is to keep it simple, but this does not mean that it is easy or that no training is necessary. Also, it does not follow that only the manager or supervisor is going to be involved in preparing written communications. In the US world especially, staff at all levels need to pass on information in written form, e.g. in response to an enquiry; in internal and external correspondence; in the preparation of a newsletter or bulletin. Again instruction is essential if the outcome is to be successful. The key to success in communication lies in being able to put yourself in the recipients' shoes how are they likely to respond to the communication? Staff receiving training in this area should be encouraged to follow that approach by asking themselves two questions about every written communication:

Does the recipient need it? And is it in the form that he or she is likely to want it, or that would be most helpful? This will provide a starting point for trainees from which to move on to matters of length and style, on which you will be briefing and guiding them, working through first drafts with them. They should also be encouraged to consult the procedures manual for details of any house-style requirements and to look at examples of various communications serving a similar purpose, perhaps produced by other organizations.

A lot can be learned by scrutinizing the variety of styles in which regular library newsletters and information bulletins are produced - the trainee will also be developing their critical ability in noting the aspects that appeal as well as those which would not be appropriate to their own organization.

Writing can also be carried out as a group activity, with significant benefits in terms of job satisfaction, motivation and teamwork, as shown in another example from Stoy Hayward. Having set up the information service, it was appropriate to write a guide for users-mainly employees - describing the range of services which had been developed, with the guide organized in such a way that it could be used as a quick direct source of reference. It was also intended to reproduce it in client booklets so that they too could be made aware of the potential' of the firm's information resource as an additional service available to them. Information staff drew up a list of the most appropriate headings, given the purpose of the guide, and then individuals prepared entries on their particular subject areas, which were combined into a single draft document. This was circulated within the department and amendments of style and content agreed at a single meeting. As well as the considerable sense of involvement and satisfaction in the final product, the exercise had also provided some very practical lessons in the preparation of written communications.

The choice of words and the way in which we use them influences all forms of communication, but the written word plays a significant role in the range of activities which make up a library/information service. For example, the preparation of a newsletter or bulletin requires the ability to summarize and present the main points of the items cited in a concise form, yet at the same time making it punchy enough to whet the reader's appetite lo follow up the reference and read the original. The skills needed to write in this brief form arc also useful for activities such as abstract writing, cataloguing notes, information reports in response to enquiries, or perhaps summaries for any house journal that might exist. Newsletters and bulletins also act as a promotional tool for the LIS, so layout and presentation are other areas in which staff may require training. Short courses containing practical work are invaluable in providing an insight into the basics of various kinds of writing, for example business letters and report writing, but it is important that the individual concerned should have regular opportunities to put their learning into practice, thus improving and developing further.

Cooperative Training Ventures

This form of interchange is particularly useful between managers in similar organizations who are likely to have comparable training requirements for their staff. It could also lead to the setting up of cooperative training ventures to cover specific areas in which there is a common need. For example, the London-based Accountancy Library and Information Group felt that the specific approach to understanding various financial matters that they were seeking for their staff was not offered by any of the standard courses available. They therefore approached a consultant specializing in financial training and together designed a series of courses tailor-made to their needs, in terms of subject coverage, level, duration, frequency and price. The training programme is divided into four modules each lasting half a day, to allow maximum flexibility for participants to be able to attend.

The total package provides fairly comprehensive coverage and, although aimed at new entrants to the subject area, has also been found to fill the gaps for more experienced information officers. The aim is to give sufficient background knowledge of the sources, along with enough understanding and detail of the nature of the information with which participants are likely to be working on a day-to-day basis. The series of modules is run at intervals to meet the needs of the group and is proving to be very successful. This approach to training could well be emulated by other informal self-help groups.

Cooperative training does not have to take place between similar organizations, or even between organizations in the same country. As Alan MacDougall says, 'There seems to be no particular formula which will guarantee the outward success of a cooperative; it does not seem to depend on the size of the cooperative, its mix or its geographical spread'. The book in fact includes case studies of cooperative training ventures between libraries of one type, as well as between libraries of different kinds. MacDougall suggests that one factor which could be crucial to the success of such schemes is the degree of continuity and stability of the organizing committee. Another will be a considerable commitment to training not only by members of the organizing committee but also by their employing organizations. Where there is support from senior management, MacDougall suggests, there are fewer problems in taking the scheme forward.

In describing a range of cooperative projects across Europe, Ian Mowat mentions one venture which involves the libraries of the Universities of Torun and Lodz in Poland, Debrecen and Szeged in Hungary, and Hull in Great Britain, working together on training and staff exchange. Obviously there will be lessons to be learned by the organizers as well as by the trainees, so before embarking on a cooperative venture, the long-term implications need to be considered.

When the present authors were employed by Westminster City Libraries and Stoy Hayward, respectively, we felt that there was considerable scope for some form of joint training even though the organizations involved were quite different, i.e. one was part of a local authority and the other a leading firm of chartered accountants in the private sector. What did we feel would be offered to the participants, given the different structure and objectives of each organization, and the fact that each already had a training programme in place? Overall, we felt that trainees would gain a broader professional awareness in terms of appreciating the range of sources and services on offer, the different ways in which these could be provided, and become more aware of the underlying objectives of the organizations involved. This would lead them to appreciate the need for flexibility of approach and a realization that LIS applications could be transferred across sectors.

The trainees involved attended only selected parts of each other's programmes, but experienced considerable benefit in increased awareness and understanding which would be applicable to their longer-term career development. Each saw a different user community with different expectations and needs. One notable example where the elements of the Stoy Hayward approach were seen to be directly applicable to the Westminster situation was in the setting up of what was at that time a new venturr tor Westminster's Central Reference Library – a subscription-based service aimed at the local business community. Information for Business is now a well-established commercially run service. However, there was at that time a need to consider not only charging for information provided, but all the other aspects of operating commercially: understanding the business environment and its language, as well as its way of working, meeting business expectations as well as deadlines, thinking laterally, viewing each request for information in a wider perspective, seeking new ways of approaching the search for solutions, and of presenting the answers. This needed more than 'we have got all these reference books and databases - let's make money by using them more'. It required not only a thorough knowledge of business sources, but also how to operate in a business context - quite an opportunity for staff development, but one requiring a carefully thought-out training and development programme.

STAFF DEVELOPMENT TRAINING: NEEDS ASSESSMENT

Successful staff-development programs are relevant to the needs of the staff. A library can determine its staff needs by conducting a needs assessment. A needs assessment is the process by which an organization asks its staff what they need to do their jobs better and, from the answers, determines a plan of action. The process may range from a simple survey to a complex investigation. Properly done, a needs assessment can be the foundation upon which a strong staff-development program is built.

This chapter covers the in-depth, complex assessment process for the library that is ready to make a major commitment of library resources to staff development. Formal questionnaires should be constructed by someone with expertise to ensure that the questions will yield relevant, usable answers. The follow-up must be timely and commensurate with the expectations raised by the needs-assessment process itself.

At the end of this chapter are examples of needs-assessment questionnaires used by two libraries—the Tacoma Public Library and the University of Michigan Library. Note the way the questions try to reduce ambiguity and evoke clear and measurable responses. Also note that both libraries have a long-standing commitment to staff development and to well-developed, comprehensive staff-development programs.

THE VALUE OF A NEEDS ASSESSMENT

A needs assessment can:

- Assist management in planning staff-development activities
- Identify organizational and individual needs and help prioritize those needs
- Identify training needs based on the goals of the organization
- Identify attitudes concerning new services, skills, or technologies

- Identify future opportunities for the organization
- Identify performance gaps, i.e., when an individual's work performance does not meet expectations
- Determine the cause of certain performance problems and identify possible solutions
- Determine whether a need is the result of a training problem, such as a skills deficit, or a nontraining issue, such as policy clarification
- Provide a checklist of needs for trainers

THE PROCESS

A. Preparing for the Needs Assessment

1. Determine who will be responsible for conducting the needs assessment.
2. Obtain management support. This may be the single most important step in the preparation for a needs assessment. It sends the message to the staff that you are serious about wanting the program to be responsive to their needs.
3. Obtain employee support. Emphasize the positive outcomes. Without employee support, the response you receive may not be completely candid.
4. Determine if an external consultant is needed for any phase of the assessment.
5. Gather background information. Search through documentation from previous assessments that measure competence, and deficiency in service. Look at the organization's goals and objectives. Seek out information concerning change and its impact on the organization. Identify past attempts to improve operations, programs, and services.

6. Identify expenses, including the staff time spent on planning, preparation, and implementation and the cost of materials, supplies, and printing.

7. Identify people on your staff who can help move the process forward—those with an understanding of the problems, experience in training, and knowledge of available funds.

8. Identify constraints—time, cost, political, and personnel—that might hinder the process.

B. Defining the Goals and Objectives of the Needs Assessment

1. Define the purpose and scope of the assessment, the aspects to be analyzed, and the expected outcome.

2. Relate this effort to the overall goals of the organization.

C. Conducting the Needs Assessment

1. Examine data collected prior to the assessment, such as attitude surveys, job descriptions, performance appraisals, work samples, and performance standards.

2. Identify what new data are needed; identify specific questions that need to be answered.

3. Determine the best time to conduct an assessment and how long it will take to complete.

4. Design an effective data-gathering method for your organization. Use questionnaires and surveys, interviews, observations, reviews of written resources, task and competency surveys, focus groups, assessment centers, informal discussions, and advisory committees. Design an approach or method for gathering data from employees at different levels of the organization.

5. Determine if the assessment will be administered by in-house or external sources.

6. Identify the population—what department and which employees will be involved in the process.

7. Identify the budgeted amount available to cover costs incurred in the process.

8. Consider various sampling strategies. Before any approach is used on the entire staff, it is a good idea to test it with a sample group.

9. Listen carefully, avoid personal bias, and emphasize accuracy in gathering data.

10. Determine whether the information collected will remain confidential.

D. Analyzing and Verifying the Data

1. Verify the content of the documentation, identifying any inconsistent responses.

2. Analyze the gathered information to determine priorities for training and program planning.

3. Distinguish between training and nontraining problems.

E. Presenting the Conclusions and Recommendations

1. Design possible solutions for the identified needs, problems, and issues.

2. Determine which solutions are cost effective.

3. Put results, conclusions, and recommendations into written form and present them to the library administration.

4. Report results to the staff.

F. Implementing Recommended Solutions to Enhance Organizational or Individual Effectiveness

Implementation is important for credibility; the organization must act in accordance with the expectations raised by the assessment process. If no action is taken, staff morale may be adversely affected.

1. Develop and implement plans for training activities and programs that address the priority needs, problems, and issues.

2. Do not waste time. Plan at least one event to take place soon after the assessment has been analyzed.

3. Plan for follow-up after each program to ensure that skills learned in a training session are practiced on the job.

G. Evaluate How Effectively the Needs Assessment Met Its Objectives

1. Ask people if they thought the needs assessment was thorough and on target.

2. Develop a method for evaluating the results of training programs and staff-development activities. Make sure that the evaluation process will yield candid information. Make sure that this process is feasible.

3. Analyze the results. Do the results address the goals and objectives defined earlier?

4. Be prepared to respond to negative evaluations. Have a contingency plan. Know what to do in case the training efforts have failed to produce the desired results. Be prepared to respond to expressed needs for further staff-development activities.

H. Maintaining the Needs Assessment Process as a Continuing Part of the Staff-Development Program

1. Establish a continuing schedule for the needs-assessment process. Determine how often the assessment should be done and who will be responsible for its implementation.

2. Consider varying the data-gathering approach or method.

3. Be alert to changing goals and objectives.

STAFF DEVELOPMENT TRAINING: DESIGNING

When designing a training programme, whether of a short or a longer-term duration, the key feature is the statement of objectives. Look at almost any commercial training directory and you will find for each course a note of its main aims and objectives, so that you as a purchaser of any of the courses will have a clear idea of what you can expect to be the outcomes of each course. This applies whether the course is a one-off stand-alone event or part of a series. There should also be an indication of the intended level of the course, and an indication of the training methods to be employed. The same practice of indicating key features applies when drawing up an in-house programme, which is likely to be a coordination of a number of different events or activities. Start with what you hope will be achieved. This will be as important for the person undergoing the training as for you as their manager. Trainees will be clear about what they should be working towards, and you will have a set of criteria against which to measure the success of the training. At Stoy Hayward, a leading UK accountancy practice, a programme was drawn up to meet the Library Association's registration requirements, which enables candidates to pursue chartered status. This was to take place over a period of 1 year, at the end of which the candidates would be able to assess their own professional development and seek Associate status of the Library Association.

This programme with its objectives and methods can be seen in full in *Personal development in information work*. However, the important thing about it was that it was also able to be adapted for use by those members of the department who were not pursuing a professional qualification but had demonstrated ability to work in a professional way, exhibiting good information skills along with other abilities and longer-term potential. This approach of developing a comprehensive programme has been found to be successful in other organizations, of which examples have been reproduced in *Best practice*, a study of continuing professional development for US staff in UK professional firms.

Objectives should be stated clearly and concisely: it is not necessary to make a lengthy list to cover what is needed. Programmes can be designed to be applicable to all levels of LIS staff, incorporating internal and external elements and showing the points in time at which each module should be pursued and by which category of staff. This comprehensive approach has a hidden benefit, in that staff have a sense of organizational as well as departmental identity, sharing common goals through working on the same programme, even if they are pursuing different elements of it.

Training methods other than on-the-job will be discussed later, but what do you hope your staff will achieve in the longer term by following a training programme? What will form the detail underpinning the stated objectives? If we take those set out in the Stoy Hayward programme referred to earlier, they can be summarized as follows:

1. To ensure that the candidate receives a comprehensive induction to the library and

information service, and to the organization as a whole.

2. To explain the practical use of various professional skills and to ensure that the trainee is able to experience the use of these over a wide range of activities.

3. To create an awareness of, and involve the candidate in, a range of management and supervisory activities.

4. To develop a range of technical skills.

5. To familiarize the candidate with training responsibilities.

6. To develop the trainee's awareness of, and skills in, interpersonal relationships and communication.

As you can see from the above, the overall aim is to produce a high level of professional awareness and competence based on a broad understanding, as well as the effective and efficient use of skills. Although the Stoy Hayward scheme was designed initially to meet the registration requirements of the Library Association, the objectives are equally appropriate for members of staff not pursuing that particular route. But what should be covered in order to achieve this set of objectives?

The induction process, aims among other things to enable the trainee to see the direct relationship of the library/ information service to its parent organization's objectives and activities. In order to achieve this, library and information staff will need to be able to make full use of their professional skills, including critical ability as referred to in the second objective listed above - already it is apparent that activities that will be developed to achieve one objective are also likely to assist in the achievement of others. The candidate may already have a knowledge of professional skills, perhaps gained from formal education, but with little opportunity to date to pursue the practical application of those skills - or alternatively, from experience not supported by the exposure to the underlying theory. Either way the knowledge may be limited to certain areas, so the need is to ensure that the candidate is not only aware of the range of skills which they could be using, but also of how to use them to maximum effect. Under the second objective the Stoy Hayward programme lists skills relating to:

- Enquiry work
- Scanning, abstracting and indexing
- Classification and cataloguing
- Appreciation and use of non-book printed material such as loose leaf works, updating services, and the development of subject files
- Appreciation and use of online services
- Selection, acquisition and review of stock
- Interlibrary loans
- Bibliographical work
- Library organization
- Promotion of the service
- Research
- Ongoing professional awareness of new services and events
- Specialized subject work in areas relevant to the organization's activities.

As you can see, a number of these will also support part of the aim of the induction process. Other objectives are similarly interrelated, for example (3), (5) and (6), with their common emphasis on styles of behaviour, especially the development of interpersonal and communication skills. These selected examples indicate the benefits of developing a training programme as a total package - the initial effort on the manager's part certainly results in a much more logical and better structured programme than could be achieved by a more ad hoc approach, and is more likely to result in a successful outcome both for the person undergoing the training and for the library/information service.

Another key element which needs to be built into the training programme is a mechanism for feedback, important for both the trainee and the manager, not only for evaluating the success of specific modules of training, but also to provide the opportunity for (a) problem solving and (b) putting the training into a broader professional context. In the case of the longer-term programme, feedback is likely to take place during regular counselling sessions, an approach endorsed by the Library Association, which also recommends the maintenance of a logbook, enabling the trainee to measure their own progress.

In drawing up a training programme there are a number of factors which will have to be taken into consideration. First the participants and their *level of operation and ability* - the level to be assessed not only in terms of the post held by each member of staff, but also of earlier formal education and previous experience which may indicate potential as well as ability and could help determine the type of training to be offered. Also relating to the participants will be the *training methods* to be applied in relation to predicted different responses by individuals, given their varied *learning styles*. As mentioned earlier, some respond better to what they hear, others to what they see, some work well in groups, others are better on their own. In addition the *timing and pacing of the training* should be set with the individual in mind. Other considerations include the *organizational and departmental developments* to which the training will need to relate; the *sequence and logical flow* of the programme and the availability of *in-house programmes, facilities, materials and skills* which could successfully be made use of, and adequate budgets for the purchase of external elements, whether these are visits requiring travel expenses, courses with a fee to be paid, or reading matter and software to support internal activities.

These then need to be added to the identified training needs of the individual in order for the programme to take shape. In what areas is training likely to be needed?

The range could probably be summarized under several main headings:

- The front end, i.e. direct dealing with users/clients
- The acquisition and organization of resources
- Information handling (organizing and retrieving)
- Management
- Administration.

However, there is inevitably a degree of overlap, for example the front end would cover aspects of service provision such as enquiry handling, loan services and user education. These in turn are dependent on information handling, administrative and interpersonal and communication skills, the latter including telephone techniques as well as written and face-to-face communication. These skills are also used in the reference interview, in conducting user surveys, the provision of current awareness services and the dissemination of information generally, as well as in promotional activities. They are also essential to the manager's own role in staff management, negotiation and other internal and external activities. Training in other management areas, for example time management, needs' to be available to all staff if an effective service is to be maintained, meeting deadlines and handling procedures efficiently.

When deciding on the most appropriate training activities for a programme, the complex mix of skills required for the successful execution of work tasks will be central to your considerations. It is therefore worth subjecting each area of operation in the department to regular assessment - is it still necessary, how well is it being performed, how could it be improved? This will provide a method of identifying training needs at a departmental and service level, while contributing to personal efficiency and quality assurance.

INSTRUCTIONAL DESIGN

Instructional Design (ID) is a method of creating training strategies and materials that are both interesting and effective. The ID process helps to ensure that expectations will be clearly stated and understood by both the trainer and the learner. ID theorists believe that the order and way in which we present information has a definite impact on a program's effectiveness. Many institutions employ instructional designers, who help decide the best strategies for a particular presentation or training assignment.

ID theory recommends that a trainer follow a series of nine steps when putting together training programs. These steps are: needs analysis, task description, task analysis, writing objectives, developing tests, formulating instructional strategies, sequencing, developing materials, and preparing formative or summative evaluations (Gropper and Ross 1987). Most trainers are familiar with some of these steps. The most successful programs will include most, if not all, of them.

Needs Analysis

The purpose of needs analysis is to determine a goal, describe the current situation, and decide whether staff development can correct an identified inadequacy. Without needs analysis, an excellent training effort may be misdirected and accomplish little. For example, Jane, the head of the circulation department, recently came to the library staff-development committee and requested a presentation on time management to help staff improve their productivity. A needs-analysis interview with the staff, however, revealed that efficiency problems were actually related to the staff's under utilization of the circulation system's software. In this situation, a presentation on time management might be interesting but would not solve Jane's problem.

There are many methods for assessing needs: observing employees in the work environment, interviewing staff, or analyzing performance data are just a few. A more elaborate description of the needs-assessment process has been outlined in the previous chapter. The most critical point to remember when assessing needs is that staff training is not always the most appropriate solution to an identified problem.

Task Description

Task description is more appropriate for job-training programs than for general presentations. Task description requires the trainer to identify the steps needed to perform a particular task or job and to determine the best order of execution of these steps. Instructional designers have identified three classes of tasks: action, cognitive, and creative (Davis, Alexander, and Yelon 1974). An action task is readily analyzed and sequenced because all the components can be observed: A cognitive task, which involves perception and knowledge, may require explanation by a learning theorist. A creative task may be difficult for even the expert to describe.

Checking out a book is a typical action task. The task description includes a sequence of actions performed to complete the exchange. Selecting the best source to answer a reference question is an example of a cognitive task. The task description for this procedure would look like a flowchart, representing each step of the decision-making process. Answering an unusually difficult reference request, however, might require a more creative, variable approach. In this case, the task would be difficult, if not impossible, to describe. The kind of task (action, cognitive, or creative) determines what kind of training method will be the most effective.

Developing Tests

Testing the trainee can provide useful information to the trainer concerning the effectiveness of the program and help the trainee to measure his or her level of accomplishment. A good test has several features: validity, objectivity, differentiability, and reliability (Davis, Alexander, and Yelon 1974). A test is valid if it requires the learner to perform the same action or skill needed to perform the actual task.

A test can be considered objective if it measures the results stated in the task's objectives. A test is differential if it distinguishes between learners who can complete the objectives and learners who cannot. Finally, a test may be considered reliable if it consistently confirms that the learner can complete the assignment.

Pretests can reveal whether the learner possesses the prerequisite skills and can identify learners who may already possess the necessary expertise before training. The results of pretests can be compared with those of posttests to determine the achieved level of learning.

Without testing, objective evaluation is almost impossible. Testing does not have to be in the form of a written examination. Rather, it can take the form of a hands-on demonstration, successful completion of assigned tasks, or verbal reply to case-study presentations. Whatever format is used, correct test design must be based on the stated objectives. In Example 1 under Step 4 above, the best test would determine the level of accuracy and the time it took to complete the interlibrary loan work form.

Formulating Instructional Strategies

Instructional strategies should be based on the type of skill required to complete the new task or assignment. Skills generally fall into three categories: cognitive, attitudinal, or motor. Cognitive skills, which involve knowledge and perception, might successfully be taught using traditional classroom techniques, such as lecturing, reading, and discussion. An attitudinal skill, such as a helpful public-service demeanor, might best be taught by role-playing activities rather than a lecture. Motor skills, such as using the computer, usually are taught more effectively by hands-on instruction than by reading a text.

Formative or Summative Evaluation

Two types of evaluation, formative and summative, are part of the design process. Formative evaluation, which is used less often because of time constraints, involves testing the training program initially on a small group, then revising it if necessary before it is implemented on a wider scale.

Summative evaluation, which is used more frequently, examines whether the training's objectives are worthwhile, identifies unexpected outcomes not specified in the objectives, and compares the outcome with standardized test results. Brief surveys which ask participants to rate the presentation sometimes fall short of a complete summative evaluation. According to Leslie J. Briggs (1977), summative evaluations should also measure the likelihood of trainees to use the materials in real situations and compare costs of different training methods. Ideally, the summative evaluation is completed by an independent evaluator.

Sequencing

Once the general model of instruction is selected, the trainer must determine the appropriate sequence in which to present new concepts. One sequencing approach defined by Gagne includes the following steps: gaining the learner's attention; stimulating recall of prerequisite material; presenting a stimulus; providing guidance; and encouraging performance, feedback, assessment, and retention (Gagne and Driscoll 1988). A trainer who varies the instructional model and sequence according to the type and level of required learning will be more successful than the trainer who sticks to a single formula.

Task Analysis

Robert M. Gagne (1985) assumed that identifiable subskills are necessary before a trainee can learn a new skill. A word-processing trainee, for example, needs to know how to operate a basic keyboard, or should be trained to do so, before learning to use word-processing software. Task analysis clarifies the participant's existing level of knowledge and abilities in relation to the targeted skill level. In other words, the trainer should first confirm that the trainees possess all the prerequisite knowledge to understand the presentation.

A program designed to teach the application of several management theories, for example, would require that participants have some knowledge of the theoretical framework on which these applications are based. Requiring participants to read some descriptive material before attending such a session would help to ensure that the participants have the prerequisite level of knowledge to understand the program.

Writing Objectives

Once tasks are analyzed, the trainer or manager should formulate objectives based on the type of mental activity required to learn the new skill. Gagne's definition of learning outcomes—verbal information, intellectual skill, cognitive strategy, attitude, or motor skill—represents different levels of performance. For example, memorizing a series of definitions is one level of skill, while solving a problem in a creative way requires different capabilities. Classifying the required type of learning improves the likelihood that the objectives will accurately reflect the expectations.

Written objectives should include action verbs such as "describe," "solve," or "list." The objectives should mention constraints or environmental factors which might impede progress, and should specify measurable results. Below are two examples of written objectives. In Example 1 the results can be measured by assigning the learner the task and determining if it was completed correctly. Example 2 is vague and fails to specify precisely what is expected of the learner.

Developing Materials

Once the general strategy is determined, the trainer needs to design or select appropriate and effective teaching materials. Researchers have determined that certain learning traits, such as aptitude, anxiety level, spatial ability, mastery of study skills, and motivation, can alter the impact of certain training materials (Tobias 1987). Libraries faced with limited time and resources may find it difficult to conduct a thorough analysis of these traits. At very least, material design should take into account the type of skill required—attitudinal, cognitive, or motor.

IDENTIFYING STAFF TRAINING AND REQUIREMENTS

Planning any programme of training and development needs careful thought and must be based on identified needs. If there has been no previous training policy for LIS staff, then a good way of starting would be to have a departmental meeting. If you offer your library service throughout the day, as favoured by most organizations, then you may need to ask your staff if they would be prepared to stay on after work for such a discussion. Another possibility is to run the meeting twice for half the staff at a time - this could be particularly appropriate where job sharing or other forms of part-time or shift work operate. This format will require detailed recording and feedback from the manager, who will also need to coordinate the main outcomes of each meeting.

The same open form of exchange could be equally useful even when there is an existing departmental policy, for example for the newly appointed manager it presents an opportunity to interact with staff outside the department without the usual operational constraints. It allows the manager to see the staff as a team and to observe relationships and assess possible similarities and differences in training needs. It provides a forum within which to exchange information about future potential developments within the organization, and their subsequent impact on the department. Such meetings need to be carefully handled if they are to allow people to contribute freely, while ensuring that all essential items are covered in the time allocated; skilled structuring and control of the meeting is vital.

The outcome of this meeting or meetings should be summarized as a series of main points and circulated to all LIS staff to help them consider their own individual training needs, and perhaps in clarifying where and how their roles fit into the team, the department and the organization. It is also a good idea to send a copy either to the Director of Personnel and Training or to any senior executive who may have ultimate responsibility for US matters. This will (a) inform them, underlining the importance of US training and development in an organizational context, and (b) demonstrate your own commitment as a manager to training and development. The next stage would be a series of meetings between individuals and the manager, in which the process of identifying individual needs would take place. The list of points developed from the initial meeting should serve as a useful starting point for these sessions, avoiding the need for a ground-clearing exercise and putting the discussion into a sharper focus.

The Role of Appraisal and Assessment

Identification of training needs usually forms part of the appraisal process where, following discussion of the individual's achievements, level of job satisfaction and areas of concern, the individual and the manager will jointly discuss the ways in which the latter may be resolved. This is likely to include the identification of certain training needs. Of course, not all areas of concern will be resolved by training alone: they could equally require a counselling element or one of the many other means of individual development, examples of which are listed in Section 5 of the second Glasgow case study, which follows. It should also be remembered that not all problems are brought about by the actions of the trainee; they could just as easily be attributable to organizational policies or procedures.

The appraisal, described in Part One as an essential element of good overall personnel practice, is an important factor in the training and development process. The identification of training needs may take place within a single appraisal interview, or may be a follow-up to the main interview. Whichever way you choose to organize this, meetings between individual members of staff and the manager need to be arranged in advance, written into the diary, and treated with the importance they deserve. It is essential that the manager and the member of staff have a short discussion at the time of arranging the date, about the purpose of the forthcoming meeting and what each needs to think about in advance. A questionnaire or checklist might help in the preparation. It is quite common practice to use a standard 'self-where and how their roles fit into the team, the department and the organization.

It is also a good idea to send a copy either to the Director of Personnel and Training or to any senior executive who may have ultimate responsibility for US matters. This will (a) inform them, underlining the importance of US training and development in an organizational context, and (b) demonstrate your own commitment as a manager to training and development. The next stage would be a series of meetings between individuals and the manager, in which the process of identifying individual needs would take place. The list of points developed from the initial meeting should serve as a useful starting point for these sessions, avoiding the need for a ground-clearing exercise and putting the discussion into a sharper focus.

The Role of Appraisal and Assessment

Identification of training needs usually forms part of the appraisal process where, following discussion of the individual's achievements, level of job satisfaction and areas of concern, the individual and the manager will jointly discuss the ways in which the latter may be resolved. This is likely to include the identification of certain training needs. Of course, not all areas of concern will be resolved by training alone: they could equally require a counselling element or one of the many other means of individual development, examples of which are listed in Section 5 of the second Glasgow case study, which follows. It should also be remembered that not all problems are brought about by the actions of the trainee; they could just as easily be attributable to organizational policies or procedures.

The appraisal, described in Part One as an essential element of good overall personnel practice, is an important factor in the training and development process. The identification of training needs may take place within a single appraisal interview, or may be a follow-up to the main interview.

Whichever way you choose to organize this, meetings between individual members of staff and the manager need to be arranged in advance, written into the diary, and treated with the importance they deserve. It is essential that the manager and the member of staff have a short discussion at the time of arranging the date, about the purpose of the forthcoming meeting and what each needs to think about in advance. A questionnaire or checklist might help in the preparation. It is quite common practice to use a standard 'self- appraisal' form which can help structure the thoughts of the individual and provide a basis for discussion. These could be modified to suit departmental needs and have a supplementary checklist specifically designed to act as a training action plan, of which both the individual concerned and the manager will keep a copy. Most standard appraisal forms have a section relating to training and development needs.

The training and development plan shown in the first Glasgow City Libraries case study makes regular reference to the related Employee Assessment and Development Scheme. This is a scheme which operates in all departments of the City of Glasgow's local authority. To ensure that the scheme operates efficiently and that staff receive consistency of approach, a handbook is provided to guide supervisors and managers in how to carry out their assessment and development responsibilities. Extracts from the handbook form the next case study.

CASE STUDY : GLASGOW CITY LIBRARIES II

Statement of Intent

Every employee of Glasgow District Council must, as a condition of their employment, undertake a personal assessment and development interview with their immediate supervisor at least once a year. The Council fully recognizes that its efficiency and effectiveness is dependent upon a high standard of employee performance. Accordingly, the assessment and development of employees will be a priority throughout all departments of the Council.

The scheme aims to ensure that:

(a) employees clearly understand what is expected of them in their job and have an opportunity to agree key tasks and performance standards with their managers;

(b) the performance of employees in their- jobs is reviewed regularly on a joint basis between managers and subordinates;

(c) employees' development activities fully reflect the Council's wider corporate policies and objectives;

(d) employees receive the training and development they need to improve their current job performance and to prepare them for their future careers;

(e) employees whose performance continues to be unsatisfactory will be given assistance by means of counselling.

The Council agrees that the process of assessment will not be used to initiate disciplinary action which should be handled under separate procedures. The scheme is not linked to pay.

Purpose

The main purpose of the scheme is to ensure high standards of employee performance by means of:

(a) setting clear tasks and standards of performance;

(b) regularly reviewing progress towards them;

(c) identifying and meeting training and development needs;

(d) improving communication;

(e) increasing motivation through regular feedback.

The Assessment and Development form

Before going on to explain the assessment and development process in detail it is necessary to provide a brief description of the assessment and development form.

It is intended that Employee Assessment and Development should operate as a joint process between post-holders and reporting officers. Each should therefore have an opportunity to set out their views about the information required by the form prior to the assessment and development interview at which the final version of the form will be agreed.

The form has five main sections:

Section 1 - Task and target review

The key areas of responsibility agreed at the previous year's assessment interview are listed in order of priority. This involves taking the items listed at Section 3 on' the form for the previous year and transferring them to Section 1 of the new assessment form. It is accepted that external pressures and constraints or changes in priorities may affect the achievement of these tasks. They may therefore be an amended list compared to that originally set.

Section 2 - Performance

In this section postholder and reporting officer review the previous year's performance in relation to the tasks and targets set. It is important that both parties are as explicit as possible about the level of performance achieved. Performance above the standard set should be specifically highlighted and the reasons for this discussed as should any areas of performance below the standard set.

Section 3 - Tasks and targets for the coming year

It is important that this part of the form is completed well, for the success of the scheme will depend on clear, realistic and assessable tasks being set.

The intention is that the postholder and reporting officer should discuss and agree the tasks and targets for the coming year and put these as far as possible in order of priority. This is not intended to be a full job description but to highlight those key tasks that are essential to the performance of an individual's job. They should provide a clear understanding of the postholder's responsibilities. Must will be tasks that continue from year to year and which are necessary to maintain the service being provided. A minority may be new tasks reflecting the need to develop a new emphasis within the job.

Tasks should be written so that they not only describe the activities being carried out but also the desired outcomes arising from them. The outcomes must, however be within the control of the postholder.

A task should, if possible, consist of a single sentence constructed around three elements: a verb, an object of action and a result. They should be realistic, as specific as possible, readily understandable and imply a means of measurement. Some examples are provided at the end of this note.

Targets should be established for each task. There may be more than one target per task. Targets may be related to quantity or quality. Targets should be measurable wherever possible. Typical measures might be completion dates, production levels, rates of return, activity levels, defect levels, complaints, backlog, response time or meeting financial targets.

Not all tasks can be measured objectively. In some cases a judgement may have to be made regarding the performance level achieved. In such cases the reasons for a particular judgement being made should be openly and fully discussed between postholder and reporting officer at the assessment interview.

The tasks and targets of postholders and reporting officers must be properly related to each other. A single task of a superior may give rise to several distinct tasks among subordinates. Care should be taken that tasks for the same result are not carried elsewhere in the organisation.

Managers of staff within the assessment and development scheme should always have as one of their key tasks the completion of assessment interviews and implementation of agreed development activities.

Section 4 - Future development needs

This section should take account not only of the training and development needs highlighted by performance in the previous year but also any such needs arising from the tasks and targets set for the coming year. Reference should be made to the checklist below Section 4 on the assessment form. It directs attention to some of the main attributes and skills that are likely to have relevance to job performance. [These have been listed below as the form has not been reproduced]

job knowledge	technical competence
developing subordinates	planning & organisation
motivating others	coping with change
quality management	sensitivity/tact
communication skills	decision-making
assertiveness	leadership
service to customers	delegation
personal relationships	financial awareness
marketing	

Postholder and reporting officer should try to agree what skills and attributes are of particular relevance to the job under discussion.

There may be some aspects of performance that can be improved by other management action in support of the postholder (e.g. the provision of additional equipment or finance) and this can be discussed and recorded at this stage.

Section 5 - Development plan

In this section details of the actions to be taken to develop the postholder during the coming year should be set out. It should be remembered that there is a wide variety of ways of meeting the training and development needs of staff. Reference should be made to the checklist below Section 5 of the assessment form which highlights some of the main ways in which employees can be trained and developed. [As the form has not been reproduced the checklist is given here.)

work experience	presentations	reading
seminars	working parties	coaching
secondments	open learning	courses/conferences
projects	job swaps	visits
user groups	further education	private study

Training should take place when learning on the job is either impossible or likely to be too slow or ineffective. Training will improve job performance if it meets a real job-related need. This section of the assessment form is also the place to plan further education provision if this is seen as relevant.

Having worked through the form during the interview a definitive version is completed and signed by both the postholder and the reporting officer. If agreement is not possible this must be recorded at the relevant points on the form.

The Assessment and Development Process

The assessment and development process will normally be completed within the period 1 February to 30 April each year unless other arrangements are agreed with the Director of Personnel.

Each department will produce a timetable for implementation before 1 February each year.

Stage 1 - Independent Analysis and Assessment

The first stage comprises the following steps:

(a) The postholder (the member of staff concerned) independently makes a self assessment using the self-assessment form to prompt ideas. This involves looking back to Section 3 of the form for the previous year and transferring the agreed tasks and targets to Section 1 of the new form (if there has been no previous assessment proceed immediately to Section 3). The postholder then prepares his or her views on whether the tasks and targets have been achieved (Section 2). Next comes a preliminary view by the post- holder about the key tasks and targets for the coming year (Section 3) followed by a review of their own development needs (Section 4).

(b) The reporting officer (the immediate supervisor) at the same time undertakes a similar independent assessment prior to the assessment interview.

(c) The postholder and the reporting officer exchange forms for each to consider the other's assessment prior to the assessment interview.

Stage 2 - Joint analysis and assessment

Having made their own analysis and assessment the postholder and reporting officer meet together to openly discuss their views on past performance, agree tasks and targets for the coming year and identify training and development needs. This involves completion of the assessment form which should be signed by postholder and reporting officer. It should be remembered that effective interviews will require both participants to:

PREPARE CONCENTRATE OF PERFORMANCE NOT PERSONALITY AGREE OBJECTIVES

An effective interview will also require the reporting officer to:

Listen and Ask Questions

Assessment and development interviews should be conducted in private and away from interruptions.

Stage 3 - Review by the reporting officer's supervisor

At the conclusion of the assessment interview postholder and reporting officer should take copies of the agreed and signed form and forward the original to the countersigning officer.

The role of the countersigning officer is to:

(a) confirm that the agreed tasks and targets are appropriate;

(b) ensure fairness and consistency in the application of the assessment process;

(c) resolve any outstanding areas of disagreement.

In the event of a postholder feeling aggrieved after completion of this process he or she may appeal to the head of Department. In the unlikely event of no agreement being possible at that stage the postholder may invoke the Council's grievance procedure.

Countersigned forms should normally be returned to the postholder and reporting officer within two weeks.

Stage 4 - Retention of forms

As with all personnel records the assessment form is confidential. The postholder retains a copy of the form. A copy of the Development Plan portion of the form (Section 5) should be forwarded to the member of staff responsible for the Departmental Training Plan so that it may be taken account of there.

Assessment and development forms will not be used by reporting officers or countersigning officers as references in respect of job applications by employees.

Managing the Scheme

An Assessment and Development Scheme is not something that can be installed and left to run itself. People's skills in running the scheme will improve over time and the benefits will increase correspondingly. In addition managers will need to monitor the operation of the scheme and improve and develop it when necessary. For that reason each department of the Council should review its experience of the scheme annually.

The handbook continues with a note about the importance of effective communication in the assessment and development process. This has been incorporated in the following summary.

The' annual review should, in communication terms:

- *summarise* all major points embraced by formal discussion
- *allow* thorough examination of the situation from both points of view
- *allow* jobholders to understand their manager's view of how they have performed and what is expected of them
- *help* to discuss and define needs for development, training and experience.

Its success therefore hinges on the principles of:

Objectivity on the part of the assessor and the jobholder.

Two-way communication and all that this involves.

Discussions which are treated in confidence by both parties.

Agreement by both parties on subsequent follow-up action.

[The note continues with some hints on the use of non-verbal behaviour, stressing the importance of listening and of minimising distractions. It then continues with examples of good spoken communication techniques to achieve desired results, e.g. the use of open-ended questions, probing, encouraging. The importance of conveying understanding is also emphasised. Guidance is also given on the selection of appropriate and specific verbs with examples of those found most helpful in describing key tasks. These are then set into context with further examples, two of which are reproduced below.]

Format of sentence:

VERB.........SUBJECT OF ACTION.........DESIRED RESULT

e.g. Provide . . . training courses ... to ensure the competence of first time managers.

Assess . . . trainee work performance ... to identify the extent of further training needs.

(This section of the handbook concludes with a useful summary of the basic rules of assessment interviewing as set out below.)

The above case study illustrates the information necessary to build up a complete picture from which training and development needs can be identified.

As has already been said, the necessary training identified may be task-oriented or person-oriented; it could be on-the-job, self-study or course-based. The methods and techniques, which are described in more detail in a later chapter, need to be carefully chosen with the individual in mind. People respond in different ways to the presentation of information: some learn better by seeing, others by listening; some from reading or working on their own, others in a group setting with an appropriate expert on call to answer questions.

This is something which is not always easy to assess until you know a person reasonably well and are able to judge more accurately those approaches likely to result in a positive outcome. Even then, extraneous factors may well influence a person's response to training at any point in time.

Interviewing	Skills Basic Rules
1. Be Prepared Study	Be familiar with postholder's past history relevant documents Appropriate seating arrangements No disturbance
2. Establish the Right Atmosphere	Ice breaker/conversation unrelated to interview Outline objectives & structure of interview Emphasise this is a joint discussion
3. Follow a Pattern	Listen & provide feedback Use structure of form to guide discussion Investigate specific examples Assist postholder to identify problem areas Give recognition for a job well done
4. Encourage Frank Discussion	Reporting officer always controls situation Discuss results, targets, difficulties, aspirations Adopt constructive approach, ask open questions Identify training & development needs Obtain commitment to agreed tasks & targets Both participants to be fully objective
5. Decide Action	Motivate postholder to perform to best ability Postholder to be clear on action required Form to be agreed & signed by both parties

It is good practice to involve other members of the team in the training process, allowing them to pass on their own specialist expertise: for example, if one member of staff exhibits particularly good telephone skills, they could be encouraged to develop a short training session on telephone techniques, and to carry out training on that topic for the department. This would in turn give them a sense of responsibility and achievement and a feeling of making a valuable contribution to the department and the organization. However, this must be done in a structured way with careful selection of the areas and individuals appropriate to such a method, otherwise bad habits as well as good can be passed on.

Having identified individual needs, your next step as manager is to see how these can best be implemented as part of an overall plan for the department. Some areas may well be best covered in-house, either within the department or through training available centrally within the organization. By setting up a programme where each person knows that, as they attain a certain stage, they will be attending a particular in-house course, considerable benefits are likely to occur both in terms of bringing about cohesiveness within the department and allowing the individuals concerned to make wider contacts throughout the organization. The spin-off in terms of increasing awareness about the LIS and what it can do should also not be overlooked.

If you are considering the use of external courses how do you set about identifying them and, even more important, evaluating them? Most professional associations organize a variety of training activities, as well as maintaining directories and databases of courses available from other agencies. Special-interest groups, either affiliated to the professional bodies or operating independently, also arrange conferences, seminars and other events relevant to the training process. There has been an increased emphasis over recent years on cooperative training across both the public and the private sectors, which could usefully be worked into your departmental training plan.

There are advantages and disadvantages to be considered regarding both in-house and externally generated training. For example, the benefits to an individual of being able to step back from the organization and consider matters objectively, to speak freely without organizational constraints, and above all to exchange ideas with and learn from those in other organizations, are considerable. On the other hand in-house training, if at the right level and having the appropriate focus, brings other benefits such as meeting those from other departments with whom there may have been little previous contact, the feeling of organizational 'belonging' and, particularly where the trainer is a member of staff, the opportunity for quick and direct follow-up as required.

You need to be aware of the range of training methods on offer to be able to draw up the most effective and coordinated programme.

STAFF'S REQUIREMENTS

If you are responsible for your library's staff-development program, keeping your eyes and ears open to staff needs should become second nature. In a climate of openness and trust, the information gathered through conversations and observations should present an accurate picture of staff-development needs. Asking for staffs input will build their interest and commitment to staff-development activities and help you plan more effective programs. Be sure to justify all activities by linking them to your needs assessment.

There are many different ways of conducting a needs assessment. The following chapter, "Designing and Conducting a Needs Assessment," covers the more in-depth, complex assessment processes for the library that is ready to make a major commitment of library resources to staff development. This chapter offers an informal alternative to libraries that want to begin the staff-development often but may be unequipped to embark on a comprehensive plan. A brief outline of the advantages and disadvantages of a more formal assessment is also included.

Informal Approach

Ask around and get the opinions of supervisors, management groups, and committees as to what kinds of programs are needed. Listen for phrases that might suggest a need for staff development: "This isn't working very well" or "we could do this better."

Be aware of recurring negative experiences that staff may be having, such as the inability to handle conflict. Then pursue the topic, press for details, and ask others to validate the problem.

Look at performance evaluations. What deficiencies does the supervisor note? Get feedback from the staff member as to the direction his or her development should take in the next year. Does the employee want to improve current skills or to develop skills to handle new responsibilities.

Support staff members who are new in their jobs. Look at the job description or skills inventory for those jobs. What do staff need to learn that they are not bringing to their jobs?

Examine documents, such as long-range plans, goals and objectives statements, and employee-survey results, for hints on how to bring about improvement.

On all workshop evaluation forms ask: "What other topics for discussion or training would be of benefit to you?"

Establish a staff-development committee to help you collect and analyze data.

Formal Approach

There are three primary methods of gathering data: the questionnaire (open-ended or forced choice), the one-on-one interview (in person or by phone), and the group interview (either structured or unstructured).

The Questionnaire

Advantages:	*Disadvantages:*
Reaches a large number of employees	Takes time to develop
Protects confidentiality	Responses may be ambiguous and hard to interpre'
Requires skill to design	

One-on-One Interviews

Advantages:	*Disadvantages:*
Encourages free expression	Time consuming
Allows interviewer to clarify responses	Requires skilled interviewer
	Sometimes difficult to analyze data

Group Interviews

Advantages:	*Disadvantages:*
Allows for synthesizing different viewpoints	Time consuming
Builds support for staff-development activities	Requires skilled interviewer
	May be difficult to integrate different viewpoints.

2

FUTURE OF LIBRARY LEADERSHIP DEVELOPMENT

INTRODUCTION

The modern academic library has had a tradition of addressing information service concerns independently within the parent institution. Recently, there have been some radical associations with, initially, curriculum development (the Library college, bibliographic instruction, and currently, information literacy) and, more recently, information management. What does the future hold for academic libraries? Are they poised at the brink of an enhanced and integrated role in higher education, or will they suffer the fate of medieval scribes? A 1991 survey of the chief academic officers and library directors at over 250 small and medium-sized private colleges and universities conducted by the authors of this article showed that there were differences in the perceptions of library futures both among library directors and between them and chief academic officers.

While traditional roles were reinforced by many survey respondents, significant innovative expectations of libraries were expressed by several directors and academic leaders. Most respondents acknowledged that changes in library administrative roles are at hand, and a few were prepared to meet the resulting new leadership challenges. It was clear from the survey returns, however, that most directors were awaiting initiatives from their peers before taking action themselves. The survey provided some insight into current perceptions and the authors suggest that the convergence of academic officer and library director perceptions is a starting point for forging a new vision of academic libraries. The modern academic library has had a tradition of addressing information service concerns independently within the parent institution. Recently, there have been some radical associations with, initially, curriculum development (the Library college, bibliographic instruction, and currently, information literacy) and, more recently, information management (computer-based applications and associat d technology, telecommunications, and networking).

The influence of these new associations appears to be changing the role of academic libraries and academic library directors, and calls for a closer working relationship with more campus administrative and academic constituencies. Gordon Gee and Patricia Breivik have defined this relationship in the following statement: "Libraries do have a unique role to play in the search for academic excellence—the trouble is, most academic administrators do not know this. They do not plan for or even think about an active educational role for academic librarians."

A report in Research Libraries Group *News* further defines this relationship: "Libraries have been able to make a good deal of progress in partnerships with other libraries, but future projects will depend on new kinds of partnerships being forged with provosts, with faculty, with scholarly associations, with campus information czars ... the shape of the future will depend on these new alliances."

Significant emerging trends in higher education which have major implications for academic libraries include:

(1) advances in telecommunications and computer technology,

(2) changes in curricula which recognize the interrelationship of academic disciplines,

(3) increases in user demand for prompt and responsive information service,

(4) a frustrating sense of information overload for both faculty and student clienteles,

(5) a corresponding need for greater user discretion and selectivity amid the glut of information,

(6) funding and spatial constraints which limit acquisitions, storage, and service options,

(7) a need for effective administrative responsiveness toward fund-raising and consortial requirements, and

(8) the management issues associated with changing organizational structures and staffing in response to changing needs of users.

The authors of this article stated in the cover letter of their survey addressed to library directors and chief academic officers, June 1991, "We believe that the complexity, rapidity and magnitude of the information revolution has contributed to a multiplicity of perceptions about the role of academic libraries in the current teaching/learning process and in higher education in general." The authors wanted to identify what library directors (from now on referred to as "directors") and chief academic officers (henceforth designated "administrators") perceived as the current and future role of libraries and their directors, and the nature of perceptual differences of these two groups.

Role and Responsibilities of the Library

The first section of survey questions attempted to determine what directors and administrators perceived as the responsibilities of library staff and how libraries were and should be organized to effectively meet those responsibilities. A few respondents saw librarians in a very traditional way: "The primary responsibilities of librarians are to select, make secure, preserve, and provide access to information sources that are needed by those who use academic libraries." One director wrote, "If librarians are to shed traditional organizational and archival tasks, they are obviously not going to be librarians any more. Why don't we retire the title?" An administrator viewed responsibilities as including: "Organization and direction of the library staff and all policies and procedures regarding budgeting, acquisition, and distribution of library resources."

Most directors and administrators saw the library as having somewhat extended their traditional role quantitatively while not having changed it qualitatively. In the words of one director, "Emerging technologies have already changed some of the operational ways in which we support the curriculum but those changes do not at this time appear to represent a qualitative transformation of a professional mission.

Although, we are doing it differently,. we are still doing the same fundamental things." Another said, "Librarians will continue to serve as the intermediary between information and the user. While how we do it may change, this remains our primary function." An administrator agreed: "The forms of access and the media for information have changed but not the function."

In what ways, precisely, have the library's activities changed? Many respondents acknowledged that libraries still perform the same functions. The survey sought to clarify the nature of libraries' primary responsibilities.

The large majority of both directors and administrators spoke of the importance of educating users: not only collecting or providing access to information sources but also educating library users. Both directors and administrators saw the education function as a high priority. Neither, however, have the successful ways of addressing this priority been specified, nor have libraries advanced as proactive agencies in response to new needs and current pedagogy.

A broader role for libraries and librarians is envisioned by a few respondents. One administrator defined the library's role as "responsive to (even anticipate, if possible) important changes in the delivery of library services; to engage in strategic planning around collections so as to make the best possible use of available resources." Another cited a library's "anticipation and preparation for future need." Still another administrator said that the library's job was to plan "for information services in concert with other administrators."

A director remarked, "Librarians will need to interact with many other campus agencies to a far greater extent then previously." An administrator declared: "It appears the trend will be a concept of the library not as a place, but as a service that can be accessed from many areas. This is a change in philosophy and habit patterns for many."

TOPICS OF CONCERN

This report of survey findings reaches some preliminary conclusions. In a future report, the authors will propose courses of action to help close the perceptual gap revealed by the survey.

Discussions with colleagues in various academic and administrative settings have centered around many of the following topics:

(1) Have the responsibilities of librarians really changed? What is the role of library support staff and how does the present library staffing model effectively integrate diverse staff categories? What might be the optimal organizational model?

(2) Given the convergence of information and computing technologies, how might the library and computer center most effectively interact and in what organizational structure?

(3) To whom does the library report and where should it report? Does the library have a prominent and proactive role in institutional governance structures and in strategic planning institution-wide?

(4) What role does or should the library play in curriculum planning and development of information literacy?

(5) What role does or should the library play in strengthening the funding base for library and information services? There has been much speculation from many disciplines on the possible effects of the information revolution on libraries and information management, but as yet no clear new paradigm has emerged.

THE SURVEY STAFF

The authors decided to seek answers from directors and administrators, since, in common with others, the authors sensed an increased importance of mutual understandings between directors and administrators. Not intending to survey a random sample, an entire population, derived from the Carnegie institutional classifications, was selected. A survey instrument was used to solicit perceptions and ideas on current and perceived trends from the two designated Carnegie institutional groups.

The study of attitudes was based on individual and subjective comments to survey questions; it was not intended to be a statistically controlled study. An initial decision was to send separate but identical questionnaires to be independently completed and returned by directors and administrators from the two clearly defined groups of private colleges and universities, groups in which the authors of the study are currently employed. The survey population included 139 institutions in the Liberal Arts Colleges-Private Colleges I (Survey Group I) and 117 Comprehensive Private Institutions II (Survey Group II). Forty percent of Group

I institutions responded, and 35% of Group II. Most responses came from institutions with enrollments of 1,500 to 2,500 students (FTE); half the number of Group I institutions responding to the survey had student enrollments of 1,000 to 1,500 FTE.

The survey instrument was organized in the five topical sections described above. The authors did not discern major differences among the responses of the two survey groups, directors and administrators of Liberal Arts Colleges I and Comprehensive Universities II. Quotations and references were taken directly from the survey responses without attribution to illustrate, from the authors' viewpoint, a particularly significant perspective on an issue; only the respondent category (chief academic officer or library director) was identified.

Discussion of Staffing

The responses to the survey questions concerning perceived library roles and missions and staffing distinctions indicated a prevailing preference for proactivity. Yet neither directors nor administrators articulated a strategy to ensure or enhance the proactive library. Respondents recognized as appropriate the library's recognized responsibility for increasing information access. The majority desired a larger leadership role for libraries. Only a few responses favored the status quo.

The role and position of "highly skilled and educated professionals who are not librarians (often called paraprofessionals) has continued to be an unresolved issue." Several themes regarding this issue have emerged from the comments of directors and administrators. "Certainly, in academe this issue has not been confined to libraries." ". . . It applies across campus as new and rapidly changing technologies continually increase required entry level skills." Several library directors agreed with Larry Hardesty, that "as librarians assume increased administrative, information management and teaching responsibilities, they do indeed shed many of their traditional organizational and archival tasks." They will need to delegate many tasks to others who are skilled and educated.

It was clear that both respondent groups differentiated between librarians and their supporting staff, and other related non-library personnel. There are those positions which have traditionally been called paraprofessionals, that is, support staff with or without bachelor's degrees who have taken on higher level tasks once done by librarians (e.g., many cataloging activities, interlibrary loan, information desk service). There are also an increasing number of personnel who are not librarians but who are professionals in their own right (e.g., systems managers, acquisitions and budget managers with accounting degrees, archivists).

Recognizing the increasing diversity and strengths of library personnel, both library directors and university administrators spoke to the need for staff development support and articulated career paths for those who are professionals but not librarians. Salaries for this group should be reviewed and adjusted to reflect the heightened complexity of job responsibilities. These "non-librarian" staff groups were cited as an integral part of the library team. While librarians should continue to make policy decisions, it was suggested that this group could provide first line supervision and should have input into recommendations. One administrator wrote, "The creation of an exclusionary [sic] caste system based on degree ownership rather than on accomplishment, productivity and competence can be quite harmful."

In regard to librarians, a respondent stated, "The MLS remains the most important single credential for the entry level librarian, but it may not be the only credential for all positions. Increasingly the library staff composed of professionals and paraprofessionals whose education and experience are markedly different from traditional library science backgrounds."

Discussion

As a minimal degree of recognition, it seems to the authors that a term other than paraprofessional must be adopted or devised to recognize important members of the team who now deliver library services. The term should describe what they do in a primary, not subordinate, fashion. The authors note that this issue has long been discussed within the profession and no resolution has been achieved.

The growing complexity and diversity of library staffing was widely recognized by both administrators and directors. The survey returns emphasized the coordination of library staffing activities and responsibilities in a team approach. The authors have associated this coordination of staffing with the library profession's characteristic ability to build partnerships with internal and external agencies and individuals.

Library and Computer Center Relations

Discussion about the optimal library organization model has been going on for many years, but a much newer debate concerns the formal structure for the growing convergence of operations in libraries and computer centers in academe. The survey respondents offered thoughtful suggestions that the concern should be less for compatibility but rather for cooperation and complementary service. Both directors and administrators agreed in theory that these two units were or should be compatible. One director wrote, "I am in charge of both, so obviously I feel they are very compatible. Management of information services and personnel are [sic] very similar." In general, however, no specific examples of cooperative activities were given and there were many references especially on the part of directors to "turf." There was clear acknowledgment that each unit had different roles to play in the provision of information to the institution. One director described them as follows: the library provides "universal management" for [the] specific needs of clients, the computer center "information storage" for institutional needs. Another director suggested that there was great compatibility in technical applications, but knowledge management was appropriately the library's responsibility. An administrator agreed: "The overlap is mostly technical/mechanical. The primary work of each department is quite different." A recurring theme in the remarks of directors was their sense that computer professionals were not oriented to user service.

Regarding the question of suggested organizational associations between the library and the computer center, the most common recommendation from directors and administrators was that the directors of both should serve on the same planning committees and that they both report to the same academic officer. One administrator felt that the most qualified administrator (librarian or computer center director) should provide overall direction; another said eventually "there would be a single individual in charge of access to information." Another spoke of "shared resources, shared services." At least four library directors were reported as already managing the computer center or academic computing.

There were many suggestions about what skills would be appropriate to both library and computer center personnel. Not surprisingly, many administrators and directors felt that management and interpersonal skills were critical for both groups, as well as technical knowledge and teaching skills. Several directors cited service orientation, common sense, and basic knowledge of what computers can do for the library. In contrast, one director asserted that he was not "convinced that we should try to be DP people in librarians' lab coats. We are book people, purveyors of information, sometimes knowledge, once in a while wisdom, not crunchers of bytes bits. ..."

Discussion

Computer centers and libraries function, according to respondents, amid an environment of cautious collaboration on the one hand, and guarded territoriality on the other. In view of this, most respondents expressed an interest in improved and closer associations, with each agency reporting to the same administrator. The authors believe that until more clearly defined organizational patterns in academe have been established, administrative oversight of the library and computer operations will likely continue 10 be based on the perceived competencies and missions (however traditionally defined) of the parties locally involved,

It seems appropriate that the comprehensive scope of library operations and wide range of management responsibilities warrant a serious consideration of directors as principal managers of information delivery, including academic computing. This role is further validated by the library's long-standing expression of a broad institutional vision and service commitment and a long-term identity with an established and international profession. Clearly the relationship between these two important academic services is still being defined in both the eyes of directors and administrators (and surely by colleagues in computing).

Curriculum and User Instruction

Academic libraries during the past thirty years have increasingly moved from a posture of responsive user service toward empowerment of the user through formal orientation and instruction programs. The recognition of this role has increased with the growing need to use technology in teaching. In light of this, the survey questioned administrators and directors concerning their perceptions of the library director's appropriate inclusion in matters pertaining to the planning, development, and review of the undergraduate curricula.

Most respondents interpreted the question as asking solely about the library's formal instruction of its users. Several directors, however, addressed the issue of inclusion in overall curriculum management at their institutions.

Many directors, according to their survey responses, felt a lack of inclusion in curricular matters. This was as strongly prevalent at liberal arts institutions as at comprehensive ones. Most respondents, however, acknowledged that they were involved in the planning and design of courses to the degree that they approved the availability of adequate information resources. One director characterized the librarian's role as "responsive, rather than proactive."

Some administrators recognized the problem of the traditional nature (e.g., user instruction and orientation separated from course content) of library educational involvement. For one respondent from a comprehensive institution, there was an expressed belief that "faculty want more collaboration with the library." This administrator was "unsure how" to accomplish this, and no respondent identified ways to integrate the library into the instructional program.

The perceptions of directors regarding the academic identity of librarians at the departmental level was a related issue. One director from a comprehensive institution regularly taught history courses which emphasized student research skills. This respondent suggested that "the library could play a significant role in designing research courses."

An administrator asserted that librarians, as members of academic departments, were able to teach bibliographic instruction sessions in concert with their faculty peers. Another administrator said that librarians met frequently with academic department chairs on curriculum development matters. A third reported that the director attended any meeting of department chairs where curricular changes were proposed.

While generally supportive, these and other administrators' responses indicated an ambivalence regarding the library leadership role in support of instruction. Indeed, the very informality of many of the cited collaborations suggested to the authors a potential management difficulty in itself.

The concept of bibliographic instruction has included both broad and narrow definitions of library activity. Recently, "information literacy" has offered librarians an opportunity for greater interaction with faculty in the origination and conduct of undergraduate instruction. The survey cited Timothy Weiskel's remark that "there is considerable room here to plan new kinds of strategies to combine training and teaching." A director from a comprehensive institution qualified the prospects for successful information literacy programs, believing that it "must be advocated from the deans and department chairs. If it is seen as a library agenda, it won't get far. It will seem like the library is telling the faculty how to teach."

Directors recognized more readily than administrators the difficulties of establishing and maintaining effective teaching partnerships with faculty. In some cases, lacking a formal voting membership on the curriculum committee, the library director was hampered by the absence of an appropriate forum for participation in academic planning. Despite the opportunities which recent developments in educational technology have brought, some directors believed that "liberal arts college faculty [are] not 'into' state-of-the-art teaching [techniques]." The survey sought to clarify types of librarian/ faculty instructional and technical innovations as well as the degree to which libraries perceived their involvement in instructional design and delivery.

Many administrators and library directors reported that the automation of library operations (especially public catalogs) fostered conditions and a supportive climate for further creative instructional collaboration with faculty.

From two different comprehensive institutions came these comments: instructional technology will introduce "dynamic conditions with increased opportunities for library contribution" [from a director]; "with the anticipated use of a campus wide communications network, . . . faculty [will] want more collaboration with the library" [from an administrator]. One administrator noted that the computer center already had achieved an "active instructional partnership" with faculty, but not the library. This respondent suggested that "automation of the library invites exploration of instructional role changes [for it]."

Discussion

The library's current involvement in curriculum issues and aspects of the instructional program was largely unsatisfactory to most directors. Several administrators perceived a convergence of information and instructional technology in the audiovisual service agency rather than the library, even where, as is frequent, media services are part of the library organization. The authors suggest that this view can inhibit the provision of a proactive service articulated and anticipated by many administrators and desired by many faculty.

The survey responses supported the authors' contention that instructional media services provide a context in which the library's accepted expertise in understanding user needs, library and computer center initiatives in information technology, and faculty instructional innovations converge. It seems appropriate to the authors that rather than focus on direct student instruction, academic librarians need to promote faculty understanding of information management integrated in the instructional program. On the one hand library directors and librarians need to sit on formal committees to know what is occurring; on the other hand, informal and individual partnerships with faculty will give rise to new ways of assuring information literacy. Building support by the chief academic officers for the library's continued, perhaps new, role in the educational process is critical. Keeping faculty informed about new resources and modes of access is the key to their ownership of library skills and information literacy instruction, in which librarians can play various supporting roles as defined in consultation with individual faculty members.

Organizational Structure and Inclusion in Governance

The administrative organizational model (in place or preferred) was the overwhelming preference and current prevailing structure in the liberal arts colleges who responded, and a clear but less exclusive preference among responding comprehensive institutions. Although some libraries surveyed were organized on academic lines, they were in the minority and most of the respondents felt this model did not fit the manner in which library services are delivered, requiring as it does a team approach. An administrator pointed out that "the academic model does not work well for those who must work as a team on shared and common goals of service. The flexibility of scheduling and staffing of a teaching department (as well as autonomy of the teacher) are significantly different from the situation in the library." Another administrator succinctly stated: "The library must support the academic program. It is not the academic program. Consequently the organization should be more administrative."

Several respondents talked of a blend or combination as being ideal. Several noted that a collegial spirit could and did prevail in an administrative structure. One administrator said, "Goals are academic, but administrative structure ensures smooth operation." One director commented, "Our hybrid status should be celebrated as a bridge and not bemoaned as some myth of Sisyphus at the mountain of parity with teaching faculty,"

The library director reported to the chief academic officer (vice president, provost, dean of the faculty, for a position title which combined these roles) at every responding liberal arts or comprehensive institution, but five. This reporting line was an overwhelming preference among respondents from bodi groups.

A direct reporting line to the chief academic officer did not ensure a consistent or comparable inclusion of directors in the academic and administrative governance of an institution. Typically, at both liberal arts and comprehensive institutions, librarians were not made part of long range planning groups. One director from a liberal arts college asserted, "The relationship between the director of libraries and the academic officer is critical." Another liberal arts college library director extended this perception: "The missing part of the equation is 'the chemistry* between the president and the librarian."

A director from one comprehensive institution and an administrator from another shared similar concerns about appropriate reporting lines. The director worried that "too many" academic officers already report to one administrator: "The library does not get full [or sufficient] attention." The administrator believed that "the chief academic officer is sometimes too engaged in faculty politics to be the strongest advocate of the library. Only reporting to the president [directly] would help the situation."

One library respondent from a comprehensive institution recognized the lack of inclusion in campus planning groups, but believed that it would be "difficult to argue for a permanent seat on [the] long range planning council because of [the] appearance of preferential treatment compared to other campus needs."

A final perspective on the inclusion of directors in strategic institutional planning and governance was expressed with regret by one administrator from a

comprehensive university. The respondent lamented the "lack of analytical and philosophical preparation of most librarians, [precluding their contributions] as full partners in higher education." This sentiment was not overtly stated by other liberal arts or comprehensive institution respondents, but two liberal arts college administrators offered comments which supported the viewpoint. Said one, "I think of libraries as dealing with transient information." The other said that it was appropriate for directors to collaborate regularly with their academic peers in the framework of a "local setting."

Discussion

This section of the survey revealed a nearly universal recognition of the academic library's centrality to the academic program and mission of the institution. Its representation should be at the dean level of academic peers. With most directors and administrators favoring present levels of inclusion in institutional planning and governance, however, a few at each extreme asserted the appropriateness of greater interaction with senior institutional officers, or with less inclusion (due, in part, perhaps, to a perceived lack of broad educational perspective).

The majority of responses from both groups favored the administrative organization model for libraries. The authors, however, recognized that most directors valued a close association with academic programs and their faculty. This traditional association needs, it appears from the survey, to be reinforced and continued, but does not require an academic departmental organization model.

Most directors were frustrated by a pervasive exclusion from strategic institutional planning groups. Some administrators acknowledged the directors' breadth of institutional perspective and experience with program, finance, and personnel management. The authors noted several responses which cited the director's experience in contending with broad and competing constituencies. These views paralleled the observations of Patrick Hill in his 1990 article. The authors are not sure how directors can call attention to their broad view of institutional needs and their expertise in managing large budgets and staffs. The authors suggest that these attributes can be beneficial to both library services and the institution as a whole when they are integrated into the institution's strategic planning process.

Fundraising and Development Roles

The final survey section which dealt with the library director's role in developing funding bases was interpreted very differently by individual directors and administrators in both survey groups. It was probably the most misunderstood section in the survey questionnaire. A number of library directors spoke of developing operating budgets, whereas the authors were trying to determine whether directors and administrators anticipated a broader role within the university for the library director in this time of declining financial resources and accelerating costs of information delivery.

The majority of library directors said they had a role in fund-raising but with very few exceptions it was limited to working with university relations on the initiative of that unit. Three directors had a very significant role and worked with the president on soliciting donors. A significant minority of the directors responding said they had no active role. Half of the administrators felt the directors had a role, that it probably would not change except that in common with other units there would be more grant writing. One director wrote, "I think the library director's focus should include fundraising in a major way; ideally the library director should be an advocate for the library externally and that his/her expertise should be used to promulgate the library's position in the institution."

Although a few directors felt the development role should increase, it was clear that many directors were apprehensive that a more prominent role would take them away from direct management of the library. Not only did they not want that ("I like being a librarian"), but they felt an associate director would be needed to take care of the internal affairs of the library, and getting an additional staff position would not be possible. By and large neither directors nor administrators wanted the director's role to change. Some interesting comments were "made by a very few members of both groups regarding a new role that was perceived to he emerging. Significantly, it was an administrator who remarked, "It [the library] has not been as assertive and aggressive as other parts of the campus but now there is an interest to do so."

A director commented, "With the influence of funding sources comes the opportunity to shape the direction of library service and organization." In sum, financial development was a largely passive responsibility for many directors. Administrators tended to articulate a stronger interest in and expectation of library fundraising initiatives.

Discussion

At various points throughout the responses to the questionnaire, there was both implicit and explicit concern about the new things that librarians must now do, and concern that they could not be done along with all the current responsibilities. One administrator wrote, "Inasmuch as libraries are changing very rapidly, a personable and articulate head librarian is more important than ever before in educating prospective donors about the nature and importance of library development." This underscores the findings of one director regarding the importance of a strong personal rapport between the director and the chief academic officer. The authors believe that directors must set priorities for their responsibilities and be willing to give up traditional and probably comfortably familiar tasks, if they are no longer of the highest priority.

Summary and Conclusion

Responses to the broad issue of responsibilities and roles of libraries and library directors revealed a desire for proactivity, yet neither directors nor administrators articulated specific strategies. Coming to grips with changing staffing categories and patterns is an issue which has been debated in libraries longer than many issues raised in this study. How will libraries recognize the importance of professionals and support staff who are not librarians? Can librarians shed some longstanding responsibilities in order to meet the new challenges of the 21st century? The survey responses indicated that many directors are not ready or willing to take these critical steps.

The team approach involving many kinds of personnel was seen to be consistent with the administrative organization model predominantly in place in most libraries; this model was preferred by responding directors and administrators. At the same time a blend of academic and administrative models was seen to characterize library operations: a collegial spirit was considered by many respondents to be important. Almost all directors reported to the chief academic officer (known by varying titles). Directors were disappointed in their lack of inclusion in high level strategic planning. Administrators generally did not perceive this inclusion as significant.

A more recent issue is the convergence of library and computer center roles and functions. While there was general agreement in the compatibility and complementary relation of libraries and computer centers, concern over "turf was a recurring comment from directors. The prevailing view among all respondents was that both units should report to the same academic officer, and that their directors should serve on some of the same governance groups,

Information literacy and the library's involvement in curricular matters were unfamiliar concepts (and many respondents misinterpreted the meaning of "information literacy").

More than one administrator saw the locus of converging technologies embodied by instructional media services, without acknowledging its being an accepted and integral component of existing library services. The authors urge, therefore, the promotion by the library of faculty understanding of information management. Fundraising was the least understood and appreciated survey topic. While library directors would theoretically like a proactive role rather than being reactive to development office initiatives, they were more concerned about diversion from direct internal library management functions.

Survey responses revealed an acute awareness among library directors that libraries and librarianship are changing. Administrators are aware of new trends in information management, but, perhaps not surprisingly, are not as acutely aware as directors. Except for a few directors, specific approaches to changes were not suggested. Many directors would like a stronger role in institutional planning and more recognition for the role of the library in this regard. The authors discerned, however, considerable apprehension on the part of many that limited staffing and perceived roles precluded some directors from focusing attention outside the library. Sometimes this was based on the desire to continue to be a librarian "in the traditional sense."

Administrators in general did not recognize directors' qualifications for broader administrative participation. They did not perceive librarians as possessing extensive experience with multiple institutional constituencies and in partnerships with other libraries and consortia. Perhaps because of the library's historical tradition as the "heart of the university," faculty and administrators have not perceived the recent transformations in library activities and roles. Computer operations seem to have captured greater faculty and administrative attention and interest. Ernest Boyer illustrated the tendency to take the library's presence for granted in the following remarks:

"One college we visited described the library as 'the focal point of learning on the campus.' And yet, despite the idealism expressed in this statement, we found the library ... to be a neglected resource." If the institution lacked a library, faculty and students would be concerned, but, considering Boyer's observations and the survey responses, the authors believe that many academic libraries can be conveniently ignored, like many predetermined institutional fixtures.

The survey demonstrated that, concerning the library's role and mission, there is a considerable gap between the perceptions of academic administrators and directors. Similar to the collaborative efforts of RLG libraries, library directors and administrators of private liberal arts and comprehensive institutions might collectively define a more comprehensive role. The authors also suggest workshops for faculty to promote a shared ownership with the library of information literacy.

The authors are convinced that a new approach to the support of a library's teaching function is warranted, one which would allow the integration of information services, computer technology, and instructional media services. To succeed, this new approach will need to include a more comprehensive role for directors on the strategic planning levels of this integration of functions.

The survey revealed that many library directors were concerned about taking a broader information service role. The authors believe, however, that library leaders can appropriately-and indeed must-provide the vision for the integration of information resources, information structures,

and scholarship, resulting in overall knowledge management. If, as one of the respondents said, "Computer technology is instrumentality rather than an end in itself," then libraries, with vast information delivery experience and a history of faculty collaboration, as well as strong service traditions, are capable and worthy of leadership.

As some of the respondents suggested, we believe that there is a need for library directors:

(1) to become more politically aware,

(2) to improve their management skills through education and appropriate training, and

(3) to develop stronger working relationships with both faculty and academic officers. In the words of one director, "We need visionaries who seek to develop a new and mutually supportive future without bias and without having feet mired in the past . . . without capricious discarding of the past."

LIBRARY ASSISTANTS IN 2002

Library assistants' are already a crucial component of libraries. However, they are often overlooked, underpaid, and unappreciated, and a steady supply of replacements is taken for granted. As technology drives the field of information management, the importance of a highly trained, dedicated staff will continue to grow. Yet demographic changes in the American workforce will make such employees difficult to recruit and a challenge to retain. At the same time, major changes in our society will revolutionize the way institutions do business.

This article will focus on factors that will affect the relationship between libraries and library assistants by the year 2002 and the resulting changes in libraries' organizational structure, policies and procedures, and the compensation structure.

Economic and Political Factors

Due to the needs generated by high each workplaces, employers may turn to paying for me work rattier than the time of employees. Traditionally, employees have been paid for hours of work usually in a well defined location. The fluid nature of technical problems often requires the use of project groups, with members chosen for specific skills. This need may dictate a new approach to employee compensation, paying for output not input, and "... the result of this (will be) a new organizational structure: temporary and part-time workers overlapping a new lean bureaucracy."

American firms must now compete in a global market and many are emphasizing service in order to survive. "It no longer matters how much employees produce; what matters is how good the products and services are and how closely they meet individual customer needs. Because information and knowledge are the vital raw materials of the products and services produced, and the creativity, innovation and application of these two elements are contributed by individuals and groups, the modern worker must be recruited, organized, managed, trained and regarded much differently than his or her industrial predecessor."

Ruth Bramson emphasizes the importance of employee attitudes, stating "Employee attitudes have a critical effect on the success of any service program. A group of people who are burned out, turned off, cynical or demoralized, or who suffer from any combination of these problems can simply fail to buy into the spirit of any service effort. The support, or at least the readiness, of the people in the organization is vital . . . There must be optimism, motivation and energy in employee attitudes."

Women will gain more political and economic power. Since they will make up a majority of the pool of qualified applicants they will have far greater choice of occupations. As a result, they will demand more appropriate

compensation, especially in fields traditionally dominated by women. Women currently make up 93% of single households, and receive only 69% of the pay that men receive.

Government Action

Federal regulation is expected to increase, especially in the area of benefits, as is the number of conservative decisions by the Supreme Court. The cost of benefits will continue to rise, resulting in a continuation of the trend to share the cost with employees. There will be an increase in the flexibility of benefits, especially those related to dependent care.

Although the rise in the number of female workers (many of whom are single parents) has already begun, most organizations now have benefits and working regulations that have been designed for a male workforce that is not responsible for dependent care. These patterns will change, as employers seek to retain skilled workers.

Modifications will be necessary in legislation affecting hourly workers. The Fair Labor Standard Act has not been changed since the thirties, and is woefully out of date with the needs of today's workers. As more workers work in locations other than the traditional office or factory settings, and are paid for the task not the time, the Act will grow even less useful. Also, given the growing complexity of jobs, and the need for creativity and problem solving, defining "professional work" is increasingly difficult. Regulations surrounding mealtime breaks can hinder instead of help flex-time workers.

Changes in the Work Climate

Environmental and safety issues will receive increased attention including the safety of equipment and chemicals in the workplace and attention to substance abuse.

The workweek will be shorter, and employees will be able to take advantage of more opportunities for flex-time, job-sharing, and other adjustment that will help meet the needs of the growing number of female workers.

Transportation issues will grow in importance as congestion grows, especially in urban areas that are not large enough to support good mass transportation systems.

PRESENT PRACTICES AND TRENDS IN LIBRARIES

Libraries will be strongly affected by many of the changes noted above. The demographic change in the applicant pool will mean that the ready pool of bright, educated young women that libraries have depended on for a large percentage of their employees, will have many other opportunities. Already libraries are losing a steady stream of technically trained employees to higher paying jobs outside the library. Retention of these employees will require that salaries, work policies and benefits better meet the needs of female workers.

The Growing Emphasis on Service

Although libraries are nonprofit organizations, they must compete for operating funds, either through fund raising, or by convincing parent institutions or municipalities of their needs. Due to the increasing complexity of methods to access information, quality of service will become as important as the quality of the collections in attracting adequate support. Libraries have traditionally been noted for service, and one of the remarkable features of a large number of these institutions is the loyalty and dedication of their staff, both librarians and library assistants. However, a combination of factors including low pay, low morale, more responsibility without increased compensation or status, and the availability of other opportunities is causing dissention. An angry rumble is rising, especially among library assistants.

Technological Changes

Technological changes have and will continue to have profound effects on libraries, influencing even their basic organization structures. Just like other organizations, libraries are experiencing the need for project or working groups, selected for the complementary skills of the individual members. As team members, individual contributions are valued and encouraged, and the traditional pyramid structure of authority changes into a circle, with information flowing in and out. As more and more jobs grow dependent on the use of computers, creative ways of cross-training and diversifying responsibilities becomes critical to avoid physical problems caused by too many hours in front of terminals and burnout caused by repetition.

TRENDS AFFECTING THE GENERAL WORK FORCE

According to the Bureau of Labor Statistics, the composition of the work force in 2002 will be a little over 52% male and 47% female. Three-fifths of all women over age 16 will have jobs. Blacks, Asians, American Indian, Pacific and Alaskan Native workers will fill 16% of the positions. Non-caucasians will make up 29% of new job holders between now and 2002 increasing numbers of immigrants will enter the labor force.

However, this rise in the number of women, minorities, and immigrants will not be the only change affecting the work force. Other trends may be equally significant. For instance, by the year 2020, one out of three people will be age 50 or older. By the year 2002, the average age of employees will be 39 and this will increase to 41 by the year 2020. Robert Goddard notes that

"The present aging population is the most educated, most bureaucratically, organizationally and politically sophisticated federation of older people ever. With those skills and experience, great amounts of discretionary time and strong personal incentives, they are likely to become a potential political force inside and outside organizations."

Along with this aging and increased sophistication of the population goes a reduction in the pool of young workers entering the labor force. A growing number of this younger group do not have either technical skills or post high school education. Applicant pools will be older, more diversified, and those interested in entry level positions will have less skill and education. Those applicants who do have the skills and education will demand and get high pay. So employers will work harder to retain skilled workers.

This better educated, older, more diverse work force will demand a better balance of work and family/leisure time. The high number of dual career workers will have the financial security to make more demands from their employers. "The new value shift centers among time, quality, self-fulfillment, children, and general satisfaction with life. Americans are increasingly assertive of their rights in and out of the workplace."

Changes Resulting from Technological Advances

"The technologies of telecommunications and computers are revolutionizing the structure, management and productivity of the work force" warns Robert Goddard in "Work Force 2002. " Already, almost half of all employees are information workers and by 2002 the number will have increased substantially. "Because technology now is shifting corporate priorities from where you stand in the hierarchy to what you know, the manager of the future will be less a decision maker and more a moderator of a collegial process."

Most jobs are already demanding higher skill levels and more education, and by the year 2002, a majority of all new jobs will' require post-secondary education. This "... increasing importance of education and skill also will revise the social structure of organizations. Task forces will be organized around problem solving by groups of relative

strangers representing a diverse set of professional skills. These groups will evolve in response to a problem rather than programmed role expectations . . . Rank and status won't count as much as flexibility and functionality according to education, skill and professional training." There is a trend toward participatory management with a blurring of the roles of managers and staff. Employees are finding themselves reporting to two bosses: the project manager and the functional manager.

The Shift of Responsibilities from Librarians to Paraprofessionals

The explosion of information and methods to access information has modified the mission of libraries, and therefore changed the structure. According to Jennifer Cargill, "Libraries and librarians will remain the guardians of information; methods of accessing the information will continue to diversify" and, "As more routine tasks are eliminated through shared databases, through the benefits of technology, and through delegation to support staff, librarians are freed for managerial responsibilities, coordination of staff, and assignments requiring special training or subject emphasis."

Numerous articles in library journals document a growing shift of responsibility from librarians to library assistants. Paul Dumont wrote in 1989 that the "role of the library technician in technical services has changed radically, requiring a more knowledgeable, computer-literate worker with greater skills and adaptability." Patricia Eskoz compared surveys of catalog librarians in 1983-84 and 1986-87 and found indications of a gradual shift of more complex cataloging to support staff, especially in larger libraries. Reporting on a survey of job responsibilities and job satisfaction at the University of California Libraries in the 1990 issue of *College* and *Research Libraries*, Patricia Kreitz and Annegret Ogden found that even activities traditionally reserved for librarians, original cataloging and name authority control, were now just as often the responsibility of library assistants. In conclusion, these authors reported that "... our study has found a major overlap of responsibilities in the area of creating bibliographic access, small but provocative overlaps in the areas of collection development and public services, and a strong division of responsibilities in management-related activities." Larry Oberg in his article "Paraprofessionals: Shaping the New Reality" in the May/June 1991 issue of *MOSAICS*, mentions several factors that are causing tasks to shift from librarians to support staff: technological changes, budget constraints, and the increased participation by librarians in research, governance, teaching and research. He warns that the resulting blurring of roles between librarians and support staff is angering library assistants who feel they perform the same work for less money and status. He also feels this role-blurring is causing an acute identity crisis for the profession." Library assistants in the Cornell University Library are now performing tasks that were formerly performed by librarians in almost every area of the library, including original cataloging, interlibrary loan, collection development, and reference. Yet at the present time, these employees are not well paid, they have little status in the system, and in some instances their work is not even considered "exempt."

Professional Affiliation

At Cornell as in other libraries, there is a rise of a "middle class" of paraprofessional staff who are articulating their needs. The number of exempt, non-librarian positions in the Library rose from 7 out of 284 in 1981 to 57 out of 337 in 1991. Although a good portion of these were in areas such as computing, development, and administrative services, 56% of the 1991 group were "library family" positions. As this group grows in libraries, there is a congruent growing recognition by the library profession of the value of increased participation by paraprofessionals in

national associations. The American Library Association Council approved the formation of the Membership Initiative Group on Library Sup- port Staff Functions, and the group held its first meetings during the 1991 ALA Midwinter meetings, in Chicago. An ACRL Task Force chaired by Sheila Creth, University of Iowa, has recommended steps to increase the involvement of paraprofessionals in association activities. Another indicator of this trend to focus on the interests of library assistants at the national level is the new journal *MOSAICS* and the increase in the number of articles devoted to related topics in other national journals. The profession is waking up to two equally vital sets of needs: the needs of paraprofessionals in terms of recognition through compensation and status; and the growing need for these employees by librarians.

The Battle for Appropriate Classification Levels

Libraries are requiring more and more training and education in general/subject education,' computer related skills, expertise in library techniques such as bibliographic searching, and management and supervisory skills for many of their library assistant positions. This is one factor eliciting a glimmer of recognition of the high level of responsibility in these positions by parent organizations, such as universities. Library personnel staff are realizing the need to capture the true responsibility of library assistants in language that can be understood outside the library. Joseph Coates captures the elusive complexity required by many new technical jobs saying, "A characteristic of many of these new critical skills is the ability to interpret as well as absorb information, which requires more systematic and abstract knowledge." A task force of librarians at Cornell spent two years writing a generic list of library tasks to provide guidelines to supervisors preparing job descriptions. The tasks, grouped by function area, were listed in increasing levels of difficulty. The Task Lists were also designed to help in the current classification review at Cornell, and indeed have been very helpful. (The outcome of the review is still pending, but indications are positive.) Many library assistants in other academic libraries are also undergoing classification reviews. The result of these reviews can hinge on how effectively the job descriptions convey the complexities of many tasks performed by the staff. Lucy Cohen, University of Michigan, in her article describing the new classification system for technical and supervisory library assistants at her institution, reported that . . . "it became very clear that the most important part of this study was to describe the work being performed at the Library to University Personnel staff members and to educate them about the complexities of library tasks and the breadth of responsibilities inherent in technical and supervisory positions."

FUTURE CHANGES FOR SURVIVAL

Libraries, like other institutions, will change many practices and policies related to human resources in order to survive. Some of the most striking changes will be those affecting library assistants.

Recruitment

Competition for applicants with appropriate skills will change recruitment in libraries by demanding a proactive approach that involves marketing strategies. Librarians must deal effectively with the invisibility of the field, and this will take a concentrated effort at the national level. Pay scales will rise, both to attract and retain. Serious consideration will be given to groups of people now ignored or at best tolerated such as the retired, persons with disabilities, immigrants and members of minority groups. Two new case studies discussed in "Studies refute myths about older workers" in the July 1991 issue of the *Society for Human Resource Management* found that "older workers can be trained at new technologies, are flexible about work assignments and schedules, have lower turnover and

absenteeism than their younger colleagues and are often better sales people." Older workers will become valued for their experience, skills, and wisdom.

The organizational climate will change, so that different is not so often perceived as less desirable. In order to attract and retain a more diverse population of employees, other workers will be sensitized to the importance of judging by performance, not by physical characteristics.

Strategies for Retention

Retention of skilled workers will become one of the most important goals of institutions in the next decade. The cost of replacement will rise dramatically, both in loss of work time due to the difficulty of finding good replacements and in the training of new staff. This is the area where libraries must change substantially. At present, many libraries provide an entry level training ground, losing skilled employees to an increasing number of higher paying jobs requiring similar training. This familiar cycle of constant training and high attrition will become cost prohibitive.

In order to retain library assistants, two serious problems must be reversed to increase morale: low status with little recognition for their contributions and low pay. The role that librarians play in this change will be critical.

A Rise in Status and Pay for Library Personnel

The librarians of the future, especially those who keep up with technology and can contribute to their institutions through management skills, will be paid well, and will have the status that will leave them unthreatened by highly skilled paraprofessionals. In fact, the existence of these paraprofessionals will be recognized as essential to the librarians, allowing them to have the time and energy to handle increasingly complex technological and managerial issues.

The term "professional" will not be used to distinguish librarians, since it implies that other library workers are non-professional. This designation is now very damaging to employees' self esteem and morale. Other professions such as medicine and law do not distinguish categories of employees with the term "professionals," excluding other personnel such as medical technicians, paralegal assistants, and nurse practitioners.

Library assistants may have ranks, determined by the individuals' skills and experience rather than classification levels, based on a set job description. "The person, not the job, may become the most important element in determining work parameters, authority, responsibility and salary grade, the real and potential value of the tasks assigned, and so forth."

Many libraries use this system now for librarians, and a similar system for library assistants will provide much more flexibility and help with the perception of many long-term staff that "there is no place to go." Expanding job challenges through such methods as cross training, quality circles, increased participation in decisions, and job rotations will become common practice. These practices will also help alleviate problems caused by sitting too many hours in front of computers.

A Movement Toward Flexible Working Conditions and Benefits Structured for Individual Needs

Responding to a more vocal, political set of employees, employment practices will be modified to better fit the diverse needs of employees, from persons with disabilities to single parents. Libraries will offer more flexibility in benefits and hours worked, offering flextime, job sharing, dependent care leaves, *etc.*, to attract and retain employees. Growing transportation problems will dictate creative solutions, allowing more employees to work at home, or in cluster locations.

The Modification of the Organization of Library Personnel

The structure of libraries will change to incorporate a more fluid work force with project teams and task forces concentrating on targeted problems. According to Robert Goddard, "One of the strongest changes underway is toward increasing individual and small group independence and self-reliance. The concept connotes a complete reversal of the fundamental notion that everyone works for someone else. Instead, it says employees work only for themselves, that they take responsibility for their performance, progress, and futures, and that they have the knowledge and the capabilities necessary for success .... Managers and employers must design procedures to help identify, employ, and motivate and reward these individuals and teams, and to recognize and support self-reliance. It means a power loss for those at the top who design, manage and control the day-to-day activities of others.' Library supervisors and managers today are often overworked, and harried as they struggle to carry too much of the burden. As the workload continues to grow this uneven carrying of the load must be shared if the managers are to survive.

All employees in the future will carry more organizational responsibility by sharing in the planning and implementation of goals. By becoming a part of the planning, they will commit more readily to the goals and therefore more effectively contribute to the implementation. The responsibility for running a library, even a small department is already in many cases too complex and time consuming to rest on one or two managers.

An Increase in Training and Professional Development

The library profession will accept the growing necessity for systematic training and professional development of all staff. This will mean a recognition that resources must be shared rather than the present practice in many libraries of supporting the professional development only of librarians. *Ways of providing increased opportunities for continuing education and professional growth for all staff must be found despite the cost in dollars and work time. Given scarce* resources, this change will demand creative solutions. Regional meetings will increase in importance, with shared accommodations, rides, *etc.*, helping cut costs. Libraries will use more in-house talent to train, requiring staff who attend outside workshops to bring back the information and help train others. Opportunities for new methods of group communication will develop with innovations in the field of fiber optics.

Conclusion

Libraries are already and will continue to be strongly affected by demographic changes affecting the general work force and trends affecting corporations and institutions. An aging, politically astute, diversified work force will be employed for higher pay and fewer hours in positions requiring ever higher levels of skills and education. The organizations will be formed of matrixes, with less hierarchy. Employees will be compensated for work accomplished, not hours spent.

Libraries which survive to the year 2002 will be challenging, exciting, and enjoyable places to work for both library assistants and librarians. However, critical changes must occur in the conception of the organization. How libraries are organized and the role of all employees must change to keep up with the demands of technology of the demographics of the work force. Robert Goddard captures the essence of some of these changes saying, "It requires an idea about work that the employees are the organization and they have the intelligence, wit and desire to use their knowledge for the goals of the organization. It also suggests that employees' loyalty and enthusiasm are not required, contracted or automatic, but earned. Increasing the dynamism of the work force; providing for the needs of working families with children; bringing women, minorities and immigrants into the work force; improving the education and skills of employees, adapting to new technology; and forging a new social contract with workers are not the only items on the nation's agenda between now and me year 2002. But they certainly are among the most important." In the article

"Future Trends in Public Library Administration," Maurice Marchant and Mark England conclude that "... if improving service is more important to them (libraries), they will use participative alternatives to create humane working environments where innovation can drive good planning towards high performance. Over the long haul, the transition to a participative approach that fits the pattern of a modern information system will be required for the library to survive and flourish .... libraries today must develop patterns of behavior that will accommodate change, and, to the extent possible, lead future developments rather than just react to them."

The warnings are clear and the time is short. Ten years is not a very long time to make such radical changes.

How do library administrators recognize, encourage and nurture leadership potential throughout the organization?

Drawing upon current leadership research and theories of organizational maturity, and expanding upon themes in management and library literature, the author urges the development and implementation of strategies to develop leadership potential. Furthermore, the author recognizes and explores the role library administrators hold for creating the proper environment to nurture leadership potential. Successful leadership development is contingent upon organizational maturity. Certain mechanisms will only be successful at specific points during the organization's development,

The library profession devotes much discussion and research on the need to develop leaders. Libraries are bombarded by a wide range of external pressures not unlike those making a drastic impact in the tor-profit arena: rapid growth, intense competition, unstable economic base, technological innovation at an exponential rate with costs escalating at almost an equal rate. The world is a more complex place, and librarianship has a critical need for imaginative and skilled leaders to navigate the course in a rapidly changing and complex society,

Leadership at the senior level, however, is not enough. As the business community now recognizes the need to unleash staff potential throughout the organization and to tap the wellspring of talent that we call human resources, so must libraries explore mechanisms to nurture leadership potential at all levels in the organization. Libraries must continue to experiment, to try new organizational models and encourage risk taking at all levels.

The mechanisms designed to encourage leadership potential must be applied within the proper framework and time line. In human development maturation points parallel the ability to learn certain concepts. Within libraries, organizational maturity parallels the ability to develop and support a particular leadership strategy.

A particular strategy may be inappropriate for a library that has developed or "outgrown" the need for that particular approach. Application of a strategic approach at the incorrect time may produce more harm than good, potentially raising staff expectations while leaving staff frustrated and disenchanted.

This article will:

- Summarize strategies applied by leaders in our profession designed to create an environment conducive to nurturing leadership.

- Propose a theory for organizational maturity based on tenets in the corporate model but applicable to libraries.
- Demonstrate how organizational culture, vision and values can be measures of a library's organizational maturity.
- Caution library leaders to draw upon their powers of perception and proceed with sensitivity as they experiment with formal and informal mechanisms to create an environment where leadership is a shared responsibility.

The purpose of this discussion is to provoke debate and inspire further investigation. Librarians should derive additional insight as to why well-intentioned, innovative strategies sometimes fail in organizations. Finally, this essay should induce all library administrators to manage and reduce risk as they cultivate a solid understanding of the health and well being of their organizations.

NURTURING LEADERSHIP POTENTIAL

Libraries are not sheltered from the turbulence and instability of the world economy. Libraries of all types have a critical need for leaders who can succeed within a global arena. Library leaders must be "politicians" who can fulfill their role as advocates by forging appropriate partnerships and coalitions in support of their services; "innovators" who can participate in the design of information systems as the technology evolves; "managers" who can maintain a secure infrastructure for operations; and most of all, "visionaries" who possess the vision for libraries in the next millennium, and who have the skills to inspire others to commit to that vision.

Many library leaders are well aware that people are the greatest resource available, and libraries have begun to experiment with a variety of mechanisms to cultivate leadership potential throughout the organization. Some libraries have heeded Sheila Creth's suggestions to articulate an "... organizational expectation [that] moves toward assuring that the full capacity of staff talent and energy is reaped in addressing future challenges."

Creth presents the concept of shared leadership whereby staff will participate in me determination of "... *what* the library will become as well as participating in the implementation and management of that future." In this article, the phrase leadership development refers to developing this potential in staff as opposed to the development of leaders for senior library positions.

Susan Jurow draws upon research conducted by the Center for Creative Leadership, in Greensboro, North Carolina, to develop a list of activities that will enhance the development of leadership competencies among staff. Jurow lists desired leadership traits and offers suggestions for activities to help individuals realize their potential or develop a particular skill. The emphasis is on developmental activities as opposed to skills attainment. The competencies that she identifies include:

- Visionary potential
- Ability to enlist others
- Confidence and encouraging trust
- Risk taking potential
- Empowering skills

For each competency, Jurow offers several developmental experiences that can help the creative and motivated administrator provide the situation to foster learning. The suggestion is made here that certain situations foster the development of leadership competencies, and that academic library directors often employ these structures through formal and informal systems.

HOW TO ENCOURAGE LEADERSHIP DEVELOPMENT

Creative and innovative library administrators employ a wide range of mechanisms designed to create an organizational climate that encourages leaders. Strategies are most obvious during a shift in administration, often coupled with the introduction of a new management style and perhaps a different set of values. Strategies are also evident, if more subtle, in organizations where the senior administrator enjoys a lengthier tenure.

In some cases, the strategy is a conscious effort to convey a management style or philosophy, or to create a culture where staff "buy in" to certain values. In such organizations, the library director is primarily concerned with managing the culture: articulating organizational values, demonstrating a management style that is emulated throughout the organization, and insuring that individual and departmental goals and objectives are in sync with the overall library's goals and objectives. The following list includes some mechanisms already in place in many libraries. Details relate ways in which the staff member is presented with the learning environment conducive to the acquisition of the desired leadership competency.

Task Forces/Committees

The use of task forces or committees is a common method of underscoring the individual's responsibility for the well-being of the library. Task forces that cut across hierarchical and departmental boundaries send a strong message that individuals are expected to move beyond the parochial interests of their department to assume responsibility in a broader sense for the development of a product or service. Participating in the decision-making process through task force membership also fosters identification with the end product and increases the possibility of commitment and support for the decision.

Task forces provide excellent opportunities to reward individuals by giving them a chance to make a visible contribution and to develop specific skills as they work together with their colleagues, Chairing such a group provides an additional opportunity for the organization to nurture the potential of a specific staff member by providing a special learning experience.

Through task forces individuals with varying skills, interests and viewpoints come together and learn from others, ultimately producing a better product from the shared effort. Individuals learn to appreciate diversity, and to confront differences in positive ways, managing conflict as the team grows.

Coordinator Positions

Libraries have continued to increase the number of "coordinator" positions in recent years. "Individuals may observe that the coordinator title bestows all the responsibility but none of the authority in meeting a specific objective. Such positions, however, provide an excellent opportunity for the individual to develop certain leadership skills.

Citing leadership studies, Jurow suggests that "'inspiration' is the most difficult competency to learn." Jurow states that the leadership trait to inspire "relates most closely to communication and influencing skills."

Committee assignments and coordinator responsibilities are two formal methods of providing staff with the setting to influence their peers. Both structures eliminate the crutch of authority and force individuals to rely on or develop their communicating and influencing skills to enlist support and persuade others. Both types of experience provide the opportunity for developing confidence in oneself and to earn the trust of others, another of the desired leadership competencies.

Promotion/Reward Systems

The formal structure for promotion, evaluation and/or financial reward is one of the most powerful administrative tools for communicating organizational values and expectations to staff. The promotion/reward system defines the model for individual behavior and serves as a mechanism to reward those who succeed within that model. The process of evaluating an existing system or designing a new system provides the forum for discourse and debate that can lead to an articulation of shared values. The process also identities those individuals who do not "buy in" or share organizational values. The identification of individuals who possess fundamental conflicts with the organization is a painful yet imperative step in the process required to help individuals change attitudes or find an organization whose values they share.

The development of a promotion/reward system is often one of the most personally difficult processes for a library staff. The process affects all librarians, in their egos as well as in their pocketbooks. The promotion model reflects values and philosophies of professionalism and it ultimately defines the structure that rewards achievement. Participation in the development of such a model would provide a very special learning experience. This situation also creates an environment to test leadership competencies.

Organizational Design and Reorganization

Another of the more powerful and certainly more dramatic tools at the prerogative of library administrators is the organization structure. Organizational design determines patterns of work flow and communication. The structure can either facilitate movement for individuals across lines, or obstruct such movement. Virtually all libraries have experimented with the traditional organizational structure.

Some libraries are experimenting with matrix models and flatter hierarchies. Several technical services areas have reorganized into quality circles or self-managing work groups. Public service areas began with an increase in coordinator titles and they are still grappling with the best way to handle the multiple reporting lines for selectors/bibliographers/curators/reference staff. Other libraries opt to superimpose a committee structure over the hierarchy, with varied degrees of authority.

This "opening up" of the organization underscores the individual's responsibility to the library as a whole and creates opportunities for potential leaders throughout the organization to build networks. Rosabeth Moss Kanter emphasizes the importance of mobility in support of "network formation," a key concept in innovative organizations. She states that:

> *Corporate entrepreneurs often have to pull in what they need for their innovation from other departments or areas, from peers over whom they have no authority and who have the choice about whether or not to ante up their knowledge, support, or resources, to invest in and help the innovator.*

Kanter asserts that innovators often succeed because of their relationships with peers throughout the organization. Although true innovators/leaders will find ways to develop their networks, an organization can facilitate these efforts by providing more opportunities to bring staff together across departmental and hierarchical lines. Such organizations create the environment for potential leaders to develop such competencies as the ability to enlist others, empowering skills, and perhaps risk-taking potential.

Projects/Acting Positions/Job Rotations/ Internships

Another indication of an open organization is the opportunity for alternative staff assignments. The literature abounds with a wide array of programs established by libraries to encourage staff development within organizations. Examples include decisions to; assign staff to work on large projects; move staff between departments in order to assume temporary or acting positions; encourage job rotations between areas of the library; and the creation of internship opportunities. These experiences have a common element: the individual is removed from his/her regular assignment and put in a new position for a certain period of time. Each experience presents the challenge of learning new operational areas of the library. All foster mutual respect and understanding between library departments and create the need for the individuals involved to emphasize and to develop interpersonal skills.

These mechanisms provide the opportunity to develop several leadership competencies. The mechanisms contribute to the development of visionary potential by providing a broader knowledge base of library procedures, operations, and challenges. Internships, especially, and the resulting mentoring relationship, encourage the cultivation of vision. Acting positions can provide a supervisory experience for an individual whose current position does not provide this opportunity. This situation would support the development of "empowering skills" and "the ability to enlist others." Assuming complete responsibility for a project, whether it entails the development of a new service or the analysis and restructuring of an existing one, often requires the use of planning, budgeting, and analytical skills. More importantly, however, the change empowers the individual with complete responsibility for success or failure. Either situation contributes to the development of "the ability to take risks."

Formal Staff Development Programs

Academic libraries have long emphasized the need for ongoing training and skills development. Today, the ever-increasing rate of change and the resulting dynamics inherent in rapid change emphasize the need for varied staff development programs. Library staff can now benefit from programs designed to help the individual function successfully in an environment where the only constant is change. In addition to technical skills, librarians learn team building, active listening, conflict management, and problem solving skills.

Staff development programs are an excellent vehicle for communicating a management style or philosophy. Increasingly, academic libraries are developing in-house staff development programs, are bringing in library consultants who offer workshops or planning retreats, or sending staff to established development programs such as those offered by the Association of Research Libraries' Office of Management Services. An organization's commitment to an ongoing staff development strategy reflects its commitment to the individual as a unique and valuable resource.

Strategic Planning Process

The quantity, type, source, and pace of change require libraries to engage in strategic planning processes. In some cases, the strategic planning process is maintained within the administrative offices, and the emphasis lies with the production of tangible product, such as a planning report submitted to a Board of Trustees or a university administrator. In many instances, the strategic planning process includes participation of librarians throughout the organization and is used as a tool to articulate the library's vision and to encourage staff to share that vision. The process is a blueprint for the organization's goals and objectives and determines the framework for both departmental and individual goal-setting. A system-wide strategic planning process is an excellent example of a formal mechanism that creates the learning climate for two of the leadership competencies: developing visionary potential and developing the ability to enlist others.

In order for a strategic plan to be effective in the long term, staff must be personally involved. Staff must develop a degree of ownership for the plan and be committed to the plan's success. This process, aside from producing a better product, creates the opportunity for staff to initiate and complete complementary strategic planning processes at other levels of the organization. This process creates yet another leadership learning situation in which the individual can develop visionary potential, empowering skills, and the ability to enlist others.

These strategies and others are available to library administrators who attempt to create an environment that nurtures leadership potential. Although such mechanisms create opportunities to develop one or more leadership competencies, success is not guaranteed and without proper timing and follow through, the final result may be a failure. In order to understand these failures, a review of the library's mechanisms, within the broader framework of the organization's level of maturity is recommended.

ORGANIZATIONAL MATURITY—A NATURAL PROCESS OF EVOLUTION

Although there is considerable discussion of the concept of organizational evolution in the management literature, library literature offers far less debate on this important topic. Theories developed in the for-profit sector do provide a useful insight to the library setting.

One interesting model proposed by Larry E. Greiner and evaluated by Paul Hersey and Kenneth Blanchard offers five stages of organizational growth. Each phase leads to a crisis point, the resolution of which leads to the next phase of growth. Greiner calls these periods of "evolution" and "revolution," where "each revolutionary period is characterized by the dominant management style used to achieve growth, while each revolutionary period is characterized by the dominant management problem that must be solved before growth will continue."

Greiner's five stages relate to the size, 'complexity and age of the organization:

1. Growth through *creativity* with the crisis of leadership

   Creative entrepreneurial leaders cannot cope with management problems as organization grows in size and complexity.

2. Growth through *direction* with a crisis of autonomy

   New leadership takes responsibility for managing and setting direction, but eventually lower level managers want more autonomy.

3. Growth through *delegation* with a crisis of control

   Response to desire for autonomy is to decentralize authority and decision-making which heightens morale and motivates staff, but which leads to possibility of top managers feeling like they've lost control.

4. Growth through *coordination* with a crisis of red tape

   In order to put more control in the hands of top managers, there is a return to centralization which staff resent, so the solution tends to be formal coordination structures; but the organization grows too large to run through coordination and gets slowed down by red tape.

5. Growth through collaboration with a crisis not yet determined To cut red tape, the collaboration phase emphasizes team management and development of skills to deal with interpersonal conflict; but Greiner anticipates that the crisis for this phase will "center around the 'psychological saturation' of employees

who grow emotionally and physically exhausted by the intensity of teamwork and the heavy pressure for innovative solutions."

Another theory for organizational evolution is a model proposed by Edgar H. Schein. Schein draws upon the research of anthropologists, sociologists, and psychologists to define organizational culture and to create a model of how culture affects the functions of the organization as it develops. Similar to Greiner's five stages of growth, Schein proposes three phases, but he defines these phases in terms of organizational culture. For each of Schein's three phases (organizational infancy, mid-life, and maturity), Schein describes symptoms of the organization's culture, asserting that "certain mechanisms of change will have particular relevance at certain stages of development."

Since certain mechanisms to manage change will only be effective at certain stages of development, and since the developmental stages are defined in terms of the organizational culture, it can be concluded that the organizational culture must be understood and managed in order to effect change.

Schein and Greiner's models both acknowledge the importance of organizational culture in the evolution of the organization. Although Greiner's model does not explicitly mention culture, it is based upon key components of the organization's culture: management style, communication patterns, attempts to organize and reorganize to achieve desired objectives, and the desire to create an environment that motivates staff. These are, among others, elements of an organization's culture. Schein's model for organizational evolution includes the notion that culture is a "necessary glue in the growth period." Both Shein's and Greiner's models for organizational development point to the importance of organizational culture as a determinant of organizational growth.

CULTURE

Organizational culture is a very difficult concept to define yet understanding this concept is crucial to effective leadership. Schein suggests that the "only thing of real importance that leaders do is to create and manage culture."

Others in the management literature link leadership with corporate culture, assigning the task of creating a strong culture as one of the most important responsibilities of leadership. Bryman notes that "the true leader needs to be a visionary who is capable of establishing a culture. . . ." Bryman further asserts that "the absence of a strong culture can lead to severe problems." John Gardner believes that "... leaders must understand the culture. But much of the culture is latent. It exists in the minds of its members...."

The management literature draws upon the research of various disciplines in an attempt to capture the essence of an organization's culture: how it evolved and what it does. Most definitions only include elements that reflect the culture of the organization. Some say that culture is reflected by rituals (or organizational routines), behaviors (or norms), and values.

On the other hand, Schein defines culture as:

> *a pattern of basic assumptions-invented, discovered, or developed by a given group as it learns to cope with its problems of external adaptation and internal integration-that has worked well enough to be considered valid and, therefore, to be taught to new members as the correct way to perceive, think, and feel in relation to those problems.*

Over time the culture becomes imbedded in the infrastructure of the organization and may even be taken for granted. It is all that is implied by the phrase "this is how we do it."

VISION, CULTURE, AND ORGANIZATIONAL MATURITY

Any theory of organizational maturity in the library environment must include elements that contribute to the creation and management of the library's culture. These elements include organizational values, management styles, norms, patterns of communication, and philosophy of service.

The degree to which staff share in these elements will determine the level of the library's cultural maturity. Organizational maturity can be related to stages of vision; conceptualizing, communicating (inspiring), and creating the environment (culture) where staff share the vision and are committed to it.

Conceptualiaztion and Articulation

The words "leader" and "vision" are often coupled. We want leaders to have vision. They should be able to draw upon a broad knowledge base of skills and experience to describe the future. The vision should reflect an effective analysis of the current situation and clearly articulate future direction.

Communication and Inspiration

Librarians who possess a vision- are not necessarily leaders. There are many great thinkers with vision who lack the skills to articulate a vision in a way that inspires. Successful communication of a vision involves more than developing mission statements or a strategic plan.

Communication is a much broader and more complex process. Leaders must communicate the organizational vision continually and in ways that motivate and inspire. This vision must become part of the infrastructure of management as well as part of the organizational culture.

Creating the Environment Where Each Individual can Pursue That Vision

When an organization has a leader with vision; when that vision is woven into the fabric of organizational life; when staff share it and when programs reflect it; when the direction is set and all are on the same course; then, it is time to create the environment where all can pursue it. In this environment, the organizational culture is strong. A symbiotic relationship exists, in that the vision is reflected in the organizational culture and the organizational culture facilitates the realization of the vision. This is the "excellent company" where values are shared described by Peters and Waterman.

The mature organization can be identified by certain characteristics such as:

(1) the management style of the director is adopted throughout the organization;

(2) programmatic objectives are in sync with organizational mission;

(3) individual goals and objectives reflect departmental and organizational goals;

(4) management style and philosophy are imbued in staff development programs;

(5) a structure that decentralizes power through budget and decision-making mechanisms; and

(6) the existence of an umbrella culture and/or subcultures.

An evaluation and understanding of each of these cultural attributes will provide broader understanding of the academic library's level of organizational growth. Some questions to ask are:

- Is the management style of the director and senior administration evident throughout the organization, or are there areas of different, perhaps conflicting, styles in practice?

- Is the organizational mission clearly stated with programmatic objectives in sync; or is there contradiction between the mission and the services that are in place?
- Do individual goals and personal expectations reflect departmental priorities which in turn reflect organizational priorities, or is the individual excluded from the goal-setting process?
- Is the organization's culture strong and unified in order to support decentralizing power and decision-making through the budget process; or is it too great a risk to allocate budget responsibility to departments because of parochialism and self-interest?
- Generally, is there a strong, uniform sense of how the organization works, with values that are shared by all and with a common understanding of direction and purpose; or are there pockets of dissent, disagreement and/or conflict with regard to values and philosophy of purpose?
- Has there been an emphasis on staff development? How extensively and how consistently? Do supervisors and department heads embrace their role as agents for staff development; or is the responsibility for staff development removed from the supervisory role?

TIMING : SENSITIVE PERIODS IN AN ORGANIZATION'S DEVELOPMENT

It has been demonstrated that a group of mechanisms is available to encourage the development of leaders. These mechanisms include: committee st ıctures, coordinator responsibilities, planning processes, staff development programs, and promotion and reward systems. Why, then, do these mechanisms sometimes fail?

In order for these strategies to be successful, library administrators must be attuned to the level of organizational readiness. The administration must have honest answers to the questions posed above.

Schein stresses this view of organizational readiness:

> *The kind of change that is possible depends not only on the developmental stage of the organization but on the degree to which the organization is unfrozen and ready to change . . . certain mechanisms of change will have particular relevance at certain stages of development.*

Following are some situations that may fail if the organization is not ready:

- The Director and senior administration advocate an environment where change is viewed as opportunity, where innovation is encouraged, and where risk-taking and experimentation is supported. This philosophy is articulated from the top, through written products, presentations, and in recruitment literature. A major department head (middle manager) is a conservative manager who doesn't want to make waves. He or she discourages new ideas, is offended by junior staff questioning assumptions, and stifles any attempt to try something new or different. A reluctance to work with or confront middle managers may send a mixed message to the staff.

- The administration structures a complex planning process which includes participation from all staff. The task requires a large amount of organizational energy and commitment. The product will be an articulation of library priorities. In one organization this may be a successful mechanism to build consensus, work through differences, and create a shared vision for services. In another, it may create frustration because the vision is already shared, i.e., the staff already feel in sync with the library's overall priorities. Staff are frustrated by the lack of resources and they resent the amount of organizational time and energy "wasted" on talking about something that is perceived as unrealistic.

- A library administration recognizes the desirability of including staff in the decision-making process. In order to encourage communication and to take advantage of individual skills throughout the organization, a task force structure that cuts across hierarchical and departmental lines is established. Unfortunately, there -has not been a strong tradition of committee assignment in this organization. Any of the following may occur: individuals do not understand their roles and responsibilities as members of a committee; chairs do not possess facilitating skills to bring together diverse opinions; some department heads may verbalize their opinion that such committees are a waste of time and are unsupportive; or the administration responds slowly or accepts only part or none of the recommendations without communicating the rationale for the decision back to the committee.

Library administrators should not be discouraged from continuing to explore ways to create a climate for leadership development. To the contrary, there are far too few library directors willing to take the risks that are necessary to experiment with various strategies. As Herbert S. White asserts:

> *For libraries, oriented toward tradition and risk avoidance to a greater extent than most organizations and without the incentive of profits to justify chance taking, the temptation to hire a long line of inoffensive looking "grey" people is just about insurmountable. Nowhere is this pattern clearer than in the hiring of administrators for major academic libraries.*

Although, we have our share of 'grey people' in administrative positions in libraries, we also have a core of energetic and visionary leaders who want to nurture the spirit of creativity and innovation within their organizations. Library literature and library management training programs reflect an emphasis on leadership development. We need the leaders in senior positions who will continue to strive to create the culture where staff are encouraged to perform to their potential, where we embrace change and see the opportunities in the chaos that surrounds us. We need library leaders who not only have vision, but who are skilled and committed to creating the environment where that vision is shared.

3

NEW STAFFS TRAINING, SOLUTIONS, PROBLEMS, AND QUALITY ASSURANCE

TRAINING FOR NEW STAFFS

Your training programme cannot concentrate solely on existing staff - it also needs to provide for new recruits. Attitudes and approaches developed early in an individual's employment are likely to last, and if not appropriate will be very difficult to remedy later, so a prompt introduction to organizational and departmental norms and procedures is crucial and will require considerable managerial involvement to ensure a consistent set of standards across the department. Other members of the team should also participate in introducing the new recruit to their areas of responsibility and" to staff in other departments - it is essential that they should feel involved, and that they are considered by you to have expertise which you want them to pass on. This is good for morale as well as for personal motivation. What must be ensured is that lack of understanding or knowledge does not lead to the new recruit being misinformed.

The Induction Process

The induction process is a key clement in any training programme. Up to the time of appointment the new recruit will have based their perceptions of the organization, the department and the job on the limited information provided during the selection process. Actually becoming part of the organization and carrying out the various aspects of the job is a demanding vet rewarding pursuit, with those initial perceptions broadening and growing out of first-hand experience. It is therefore essential that tile information provided is accurate and as detailed as required. The induction process involves the passing on of information about the various functions of the organization, combined with meeting people and establishing what is based where. For the new recruit it is a high learning curve, requiring considerable concentration and questioning to pull it all together. This is where managers play a central role, making themselves readily available to answer questions and, where appropriate, suggesting means by which the new recruit may be able to find out for themselves.

What are the components of an induction programme? The first day's activities should aim at a general familiarization with the new work-place and the job, and in particular should allow the new recruit to establish a base. Having a desk or locker in which to put your personal belongings, as well as a supply of pens, pencils and stationery, is important. Knowing where the cloakroom is, and what the lunch arrangements are, may all sound pretty basic, but once the basics are established the new recruit will feel comfortable and able to concentrate on the wider issues involved.

It is good practice to give the new recruit one or two tasks on that first day, so that they will be able to end the day with a feeling of having achieved something and made a contribution - they will feel that they have really started. A mini-tour is appropriate at this stage, pointing out key areas of which early cognizance is helpful. Limit the number of personal introductions at this stage, to allow new members of staff more easily to remember faces and names. In some organizations photographs of staff are displayed on a notice board, often for security reasons; these can also form a useful point of reference for the new recruit, as can any brochures which may contain photographs and organization charts. The internal telephone list can also be useful in staff identification, especially if it is arranged both by department and personal name. Make sure that the new member has their own copy.

Most organizations require the first portion of the day to be spent with the personnel department, clarifying conditions of employment, providing any relevant documentation and establishing personal details for the records. General discussion about company training policies may take place here, but the specifics of the individual's training are more likely to be discussed with the line manager.

It is with this person that the next part of the day is likely to be spent. The manager or supervisor should set the job in perspective and introduce the new member to the rest of the staff, having first provided the opportunity for the new recruit to put away personal belongings, note his or her extension number and generally establish a base. The manager will outline the structure of the organization and describe the main activities of the department before moving on to the role that the new recruit has been appointed to perform. Any supporting documentation such as guides to the service or organizational brochures should be given to the new member for retention and later reference. At this stage it is probably advisable to hand new staff over to a colleague, carefully selected in advance, to take them around the department and talk less formally to other colleagues about the service.

The new member will also be gaining information by observation, for example of the layout, the information resources and the general style of behaviour towards users of the service. It can be reassuring for someone on their first day in a job to recognize familiar sources or equipment, and to be able to establish some early credibility with their new colleagues by being encouraged to participate in dialogue rather than being subjected to a non-stop listing of 'what we have' and 'here is' - hence the need for careful selection of the member of staff who is to conduct this initial walkabout.

The department must be able to continue to function throughout this process, so it is a good idea at some stage of the day to introduce the tasks you want the new recruit to carry out. Make sure that these are described clearly, along with any relevant sources or procedures, including any manual of procedures which exists, encouraging the individual to use it for reference at all times; at the same time impress on them your willingness and that of the rest of the team, to be consulted throughout. Make sure that the new member of staff is not suddenly abandoned at the midday break: perhaps the colleague who was given earlier responsibility could offer to show them the staff dining area, or the nearest sandwich bar, and describe nearby shopping facilities.

Most library and information services operate continuously throughout the day, covering breaks on a shift or rota basis. It is important to involve new recruits in decisions about their place in the rota, for example if there is a choice of taking late or early lunch encourage them to be honest in stating their preference, especially where this may be based on the need to meet a prior commitment. This is best established in the discussion with the supervisor or manager, rather than risking other members of staff unwittingly putting their preferences to the fore. It is particularly important where flexible schedules and job-sharing arrangements are involved.

The first afternoon could allow the new recruit to continue with the tasks which have been allocated, followed by an introduction to one specific section of the stock/services. It is useful to allow a little time for constructive browsing, asking questions as they arise, to enable the recruit to become familiar with the sources available. It is important that they do not feel superfluous or forgotten, so suggest that at the end of that time they make contact again with you or another member of staff to move on to the next part of the schedule. You may want to fit in another short walkabout, or send them off to deliver something to a department to which they were introduced earlier. Before the end of the day you should have a meeting to summarize their activities, to provide feedback on the completed tasks, to answer any questions, and to set expectations for the next day, according to the programme that you will have given them at the beginning of the day.

The balance of tasks, visits and introductions will shift as familiarization takes place and the new recruit begins to demonstrate a range of ability. Where you have a standard training programme, this demonstration of understanding and ability will indicate to you when to introduce specific training activities, but before this it is advisable for the recruit to participate in any formal centrally organized induction course, often involving all new employees, whatever their specialist function or level.

Depending on the organization, these may be run several times a year, or just whenever there is a suitable number of new recruits. In a commercial organization the induction course will usually involve one or two days away from the department, following a structured programme during which new staff will meet each other and be given a series of short presentations by senior members of other departments.

These are usually intentionally informal, often offering the opportunity for the presenters to talk further with the new recruits over lunch, answering questions and just generally making them feel at home with the organization and each other. From the new employees' viewpoint they will suddenly have a series of personal contacts as well as knowing more about the organization and the way in which it operates.

The pace at which the total induction process is taken is important, as it is very easy to give too much information at a time. Constant questioning and checking by the new member of staff is to be encouraged, and is essential if they are to be expected to follow certain procedures, work to stated standards and become integrated into the department.

The induction process does not end with the formal induction day or course but continues over a period of time, with the initial introductions being taken further through a series of longer and more detailed meetings with heads of various departments or functions.

These need to be built in at appropriate stages throughout the longer-term training programme. They need to be arranged in advance, regarded as important and booked into the diary as formal meetings. If two new members of staff can go together, this will be beneficial in that:

(a) there will be the reinforcing factor of subsequent discussion as well as two sets of notes taken during the session, and

(b) it will avoid the need to make too frequent demands on the senior staff involved.

On-the-Job Training

Apart from the familiarization sessions, staff will also learn by observing other staff. This should be encouraged but make sure that the particular staff member chosen for observation knows how to train as well as being good at their job. This is something to be talked through before the arrival of the new recruit, so that staff can think about and perhaps be advised of possible techniques to use, and make adequate preparation.

If well prepared this approach can be very successful, and can also contribute to the establishment of working relationships for the future.

CASE STUDY: WESTMINSTER REFERENCE LIBRARY

Another training method found by Westminster Reference Library (part of a London public library -service) to be very successful with new members of staff is that of 'shadowing'. Chris Tighe, currently the Training Officer there, says that the aim is to get a competent member of staff in the shortest possible time, whilst ensuring that they feel comfortable with the learning experience, yet allowing them to make an early contribution to the work of the department. On their first day new members of staff meet the Business Unit Manager for an explanation of the service - how it operates and what is expected of them. They then move on to a general tour of the building, both resources and facilities, with the Training Officer.

On the second half of that same day, they are likely to find themselves on the enquiry desk - potentially a daunting prospect. This is when the 'shadowing' begins. The Training Officer stands close by, listening to the enquiry but not interfering with the trainee's communication with the enquirer. When the questioning has finished, the Training Officer talks with the trainee to establish that the question has been interpreted correctly and to suggest an appropriate source in which the answer is likely to be found. He then accompanies the trainee to seek the source material and suggests how best to use it.

All this must be handled very discreetly to avoid embarrassment to the trainee, and to avoid a loss of confidence by the enquirer. It has to be carried out fairly quickly too, as the enquirer is usually waiting there for the answer. Chris Tighe stresses the importance of consulting with the trainee and not with the enquirer during this process, so that he is not seen to be interfering or taking over. As the trainee gains in both confidence and knowledge the 'shadow' gradually withdraws. Other elements of early training cover identifying and locating sources, the use of reference works and periodicals, bibliographic checking, and use of the catalogue. Quizzes have been found to be a useful training method in these areas.

Over the first 4 or 5 weeks there will be a series of sessions on specific types of material, for example those dealing with government publications, maps, law, the European Community, all taken by senior members of staff specializing in those fields. The layout of the building in relation to the location of different parts of the reference collection has also been taken into account in structuring the training. For example, the ground floor which houses the commercial and technical material and the catalogues, acts as the key to the whole library. Therefore, trainees carry out their initial training and become fully competent there before moving on to the first floor, which houses general reference material, a much more diffuse collection. Here they receive the next block of training.

They then alternate between these two floors regularly, often on a daily basis, to reinforce their early training as well as to widen it. After perhaps 6-9 months, they will move on to further training on the second floor, which houses the art library, and which will involve them in rather more specialist training. The 'shadowing' process has proved especially successful not least because it has been carried out with great sensitivity as well as being handled by someone with considerable experience in reference work.

Chris Tighe offers the following practical hints to managers conducting or contributing to the induction process:

- Draw up checklists to ensure every topic is covered
- Never go straight into a session—spend a little time on non-work matters first
- Never parade your own knowledge

- Sessions should be custom-made for the trainee, not the trainer
- Watch out for signs of fatigue, if necessary terminating the session when saturation is reached
- Don't be too encouraging—they need to realize they still have a long way to go
- Watch for weaknesses, exploit strengths
- Remind and reinforce—e.g. Didn't we look at that on Tuesday? That's very similar to the question we had yesterday.
- Give plenty of feedback, show interest, e.g. How was the last session? Anything you want to go over again? If you think of anything let me know.
- Informal daily consultation is essential.

Wherever possible, 'live' situations should be used in the training process, for example working on real enquiries, carrying out tasks which meet a real need such as developing an index or updating subject files. Not only will the new member feel that they are learning, they will also know that they have made a real contribution. One successful way of doing this is to give the new recruit a project which will be their own special area of responsibility. They will be able to carry it out over a period of time, seeking advice as needed, but also having the opportunity to use their initiative.

One approach used in the Stoy Hayward training programme was that of setting up an index for the monthly newsletter produced by the technical department. It was something which had long been felt would be useful, and as enquiries emanating from this newsletter grew, it became the project for a new member of staff. It provided a learning situation on indexing techniques, along with the need to talk to potential users about their requirements in respect of such an index. It also required the indexer to build up an understanding of the accounting terms used, which was valuable in the long term, given the nature of the organization and its broader information needs.

Where there is more than one library or information department within an organization, job rotation is another work-based method which can be used as part of training. Job rotation usually operates by providing a short fixed term in each department or role. This in itself means that staff are more motivated to learn in the limited time they know to be available, will not be there too long for everything to become routine or boring, and are therefore likely to bring a fresh approach to the tasks involved. Job exchange, although involving longer periods in the alternative post, will also bring similar benefits.

TRAINING FOR MANAGER'S

The effective management of training presupposes a knowledge and understanding of people and their behaviour in a learning situation; an up-to-date knowledge of the particular field within which the trainee will be operating; an awareness of available training both internal and external, along with the ability to evaluate the appropriateness of that training and the skill to assess its effectiveness, accompanied by any necessary counselling and advice; and experience and knowledge of training techniques and method's. Quite a tall order, and often one which is not thought through in such detail when the appointment of a departmental manager is made.

Unfortunately the old adage 'managers are born, not made' is still given credence in some quarters, without consideration that even apparently 'natural' skills can be improved, developed, built on or used differently. Many people, when taking on a library management role, find themselves not just continuing to use their specialist skills and knowledge with 'a bit of administration tacked on', but also regularly being called upon to resolve problems, initiate activities and, in particular, become fully immersed in the whole process of managing financial and human resources as well as those relating to the retrieval of information. In order to carry out those management responsibilities, the newly appointed manager may well require training in various management skills and techniques, as well as being introduced to organizational procedures in which they may not previously have been involved.

'We need managers who are innovative, forward-looking and service-oriented, able to communicate with and get the best out of other people, and skilled in managing resources'— a statement by the British Library in its strategic 5-year plan aimed at taking the British Library forward to 1994. In that same publication the British Library says that it will pursue staff development by drawing up programmes for each level of management and operation, defining the personal qualities, skills and knowledge essential to each.

It is not only the British Library that is following this line. Libraries and information services of all kinds, in many countries, are recognizing the need for sound management skills if their service is to move forward in line with user demand and at the same time make the most cost-effective use of resources. For example, the opening up of the European Single Market allows freedom of movement by professionals across the job market in all member states. This means that in addition to any specialist knowledge required to carry out a particular job, the benefits of broad-based management skills will help considerably in adapting to any differences there may be in the way in which library and information services are offered.

Being a library or information manager, that is, managing budgets, information, users, staff, and especially top management, requires a wide range of skills. In addition, managers need both creative and analytical skills in order to innovate and plan for a successful future. However, as

Margaret Trask, Executive Director of the Australian Information Management Association, said at a seminar on the subject 'managing is usually thrust upon those who show promise in dealing with staff or in getting work done or being competent in their job'. She goes on to suggest that showing promise is not enough; managers needs training and development if they are to realize their full potential in all their areas of responsibility. Trask notes some of the key concerns of those moving from being managed into the process of managing.

These include how to motivate staff, managing conflict, setting goals and objectives, and what is described as 'self-concept' or getting to know yourself and to understand your own work behavioural style. As new managers move on to middle and senior management, of course they still have concerns about staff motivation, managing conflict and the areas listed above, but Trask notes that their main concerns focus on other aspects such as building work groups, negotiation skills, strategic planning and managing change. Other areas of concern to middle and senior managers, also identified by Trask, are lack of trust, power and influence, and leadership. These areas are referred to later in this chapter. The AIMA hopes to publish a Resource.

Notebook on Strategic Planning in response to the desire expressed by managers to learn more about planning processes. This need is illustrated in a paper given by Susan Moore to the first national seminar on Library Staff Development held in Australia in 1990. In this she describes the approach taken in the Royal Melbourne Institute of Technology Libraries when planning a client services programme. One factor that was perceived as being crucial to the hoped-for success of this new direction was staff training, and for that to be effective the plan had to include training for trainers. Training is another area often taken for granted when someone is first promoted to a management position, and yet it requires a considerable range of expertise. Moore's paper provides a useful case study for managers who may be planning a new service or modifying an existing one. It highlights the importance of staff being encouraged to see themselves as part of a team, to have confidence in themselves and their work, and through this to improve service provision and delivery. This will involve the manager in clarifying their role and the objective of the new service, in setting shared priorities, and demonstrating the organizational as well as the individual benefits.

The more responsibility a manager has, the more they need positive and well-defined support from top management. This should be via the two-way communication of new ideas, encouragement to pursue initiatives, trust, clear guidelines, feedback on initiatives taken, and praise when these have been successful and explanation rather than negative reproof if mistakes have been made. An enlightened top management will realize that trust and the freedom to pursue ideas and take action are part of the role of being a professional and a manager, and are vital it creativity is not to be stilled or trustrated. Positive support of this kind can lead to high-level contributions to the organization's goals and objectives by the manager and the service they are running. The development of management potential is a continuing process which, if well-designed and structured, brings maximum benefit to both the organization and the manager.

Staff Relations

A motivated manager will lead to motivated staff. In the process of undergoing their own training and development programme, the manager will be much more in touch with what other staff are experiencing, or in need of, regarding their own progress. Their development will give you job satisfaction, while your efforts in your own personal development will not only act as an example for them but also bring about a strong feeling of working together. It will open up communication channels, bring strong team loyalty and lead to service enhancement and development. The

British Council case study demonstrates the benefits of an organization-wide approach to training and development, and also underlines the direct benefit to staff relations. Group activities, on-the-job training, appraisal and assessment sessions are all dependent on positive staff relations, based on effective management, as illustrated by the extracts from the Glasgow Employee Assessment and Development Scheme Handbook, reproduced.

Shared training and joint involvement in a particular area of learning activity can have a strong impact in producing such benefits. For example, the development and introduction of performance indicators and quality assurance programmes described shows the potential of such activities in team building. The introduction of various efficiency techniques provides a particularly appropriate area in which to plan shared activity, being something which, to be successful, has to operate consistently across the department and the organization. One such efficiency technique, that of time management, lends itself well to this approach.

Time Management

This is another subject on which managers may need to focus in terms of their own development, as well as introducing across the department as a whole. One commodity that is part of everyone's life is time. Unfortunately, unlike most other commodities this one cannot be replaced, nor can an additional amount be purchased. Over recent years there has been a proliferation of management books and articles, as well as seminars and conference papers, devoted to the subject of time and how to use and manage it effectively and efficiently. The main thrust of time management is towards setting up controls to handle more effectively the key elements of our work life, e.g. the physical environment, from the filing system down to the positioning of the desk, and the human factor - people and our interaction with them. 'Never handle a piece of paper more than once' and Tailing to plan is planning to fail' are two of the maxims regularly put forward, followed closely by firm advice to delegate more. Staff at all levels, regardless of the degree of specialism within which they operate, are likely to suffer from the same conditions, which require them to consider practising more careful time management.

Improving time management involves changing behaviour and attitudes. For example, one known time waster is the person - perhaps more senior than yourself - who drops in 'just to see that everything is alright'. How do you convey to them that they have just interrupted a complex thought process concerning a matter they had told you yesterday was top priority? Interruptions feature high on most managers' list of time wasters. Advice on how to deal with them is likely to be included in most time management courses, but you might also be greatly assisted by some assertiveness training. As Helen Gothberg (4) concluded, time management is no longer a case of time and motion study but has rather to do with self-management. She has carried out a number of studies in various types of library including academic (5), special (6) and state (4).

Telephone interruptions and drop-in visitors are ranked second and third on Gothberg's list of top time wasters in special libraries, with the inability to say 'no' coming seventh in the top ten. In state libraries telephone interruptions are again placed as the second-highest time waster, with drop-in visitors fifth and inability to say 'no' eighth. Tom Altwood comes up with a similar list in his article on the subject. He notes lack of focus as the top time waster, with interruptions at number three. It is interesting to compare this with his list of what are considered to be the ten best ways to use time.

Top ten ways to use time	**Top ten time wasters**
1. Think and plan	1. Lack of focus
2. Establish priorities	2. Poor meetings
3. Get organized	3. Interruptions

4. Be effective	4. Crises
5. Manage change	5. Trivia
6. Adapt culture	6. Procrastination
7. Develop staff	7. Travelling
8. Be practical	8. Failure to plan
9. Use every minute	9. Not delegating
10. Take time off	10. Inappropriate technology

(Reproduced by kind permission of Tom Attwood of Cargill, Attwood & Thomas Ltd.)

The above lists are based on regular analysis of the chief time wasters as indicated by more than 1000 managers in various jobs in 15 countries. Attwood has carried out work of this kind in both companies and professional associations, and is very aware of the need for the development of management skills by those working in specialist fields.

Time management cannot be carried out in isolation. Whatever the organization, whether it be in the public or the private sector, mechanisms need to be put into place to heighten awareness of efficiency potential and to support its pursuit by all members of staff.

In order for this to be most effective, each member of an organization needs to be made aware of their own use of time, and have adequate appropriate training in time management skills and techniques, and the opportunity for their continued use. Once the initial promotion and introductory sessions have been carried out on an organization-wide basis, it can then be most beneficial to proceed with the training and development on a team basis within departments, allowing problems and benefits to be shared. This is much more likely to motivate staff to practise time management and not feel uncomfortable about doing so. It is also likely to bring about now ideas on the review of a number of areas of work, ultimately producing a much more effective service to users.

Corporate Awareness

It is most important when seeking or setting up any training programme concerned with the introduction of specific concepts and techniques, that these are presented according to the norms and procedures operating across the organization. This will put the training into context and make its application relevant and therefore more likely to be successful. This is when the two-way communication between managers and top management will prove extremely useful. If the organization is planning developments in a certain direction, this will also present additional opportunities for staff development.

Attwood points out the importance of managers understanding the company culture, so that when they set about establishing a culture of achievement within their particular department or function, it will be much more likely to work. His article explains how to identify an existing organizational culture and how to use it successfully, or even change it. Among n number of areas influenced by corporate culture, Attwood notes particularly the impact on recruitment, training and development policy, and says that 'a good culture creates loyalty with both staff and customers' and 'it certainly governs the success of any change'. Working with tin' corporate culture does not win just coalonning or being afraid to introduce change, but rather seeking to make positive use of and build on what is already there.

In terms of training and development this is likely to mean identifying the degree of commitment to, and attitudes towards, such activities, as well as establishing what policies exist and how they are currently implemented. Knowledge of these aspects of organizational behaviour will provide you with the appropriate platform from which to launch your own ideas, and help you to project them in the right direction. Lyn Currie notes the importance and potential benefit of viewing staff training and development activities in an organizational context. She says 'there must be visible meaningful support for staff development with an administrative framework that assists with the organization, delivery, management and promotion of staff development activities'.

She goes on to give examples of ways in which appropriate support mechanisms can be put into place, one of which is the 'use of interdepartmental working parties to enhance understanding of the interrelationship of library operations' - another example of the way in which two-way communication could enhance the LIS manager's own learning and development.

This emphasis on the importance of developing corporate awareness in conjunction with management skills is strongly supported in the UK by the Library Association in its *Framework for continuing professional development*. In this, four key elements which make up US work are identified:

- Library and information skills
- Personal effectiveness/communications
- Management skills
- Corporate skills.

Under the last two headings a number of specific areas are listed as potential areas for continuing professional development. These are:

The areas of skill and knowledge shown under the heading 'Personal effectiveness' cover problem solving, communications, coaching and teamwork and therefore form an essential base from which to put into practice the above listed management and corporate skills.

These certainly underline the broader perspective in which librarians and information managers today and in the future need to view their role, and are very much in line with Attwood's thinking, as mentioned earlier.

Management skills	Corporate skills
• Planning	• Achieving goals and objectives of parent organization through library
• Finance/budgeting	and information services
• Personnel/staff management	• Using the organizational con text
• Leadership	• Awareness of national and local policies
• Marketing	
• Performance review	• Political know-how

(Reproduced by kind permission of the Library Association.)

Peter Senge is one of a growing number of experts across the USA and in Europe promoting the concept of 'the learning organization'. Among the key elements which make up this concept are those of :

(a) shared vision which will lead to commitment rather than compliance, and

(b) team learning, of which Senge is also a proponent. Another interesting point in Senge's thesis is that he sees the effective leader not as the brilliant orator able to mesmerize an audience, but as someone distinguished by clear thinking, strong commitment to the organization, and enthusiasm to continually learn more.

Effective Leadership

Strong leadership as the key to the future success of the US profession is well argued by Martha Boaz in her contribution to IFLA's guidebook on continuing education. In this she suggests that not only are dramatic local, national and international changes essential if the profession is to grow, but also that there is a need for more aggressive and productive leaders in the profession.

Library and information professional associations throughout the world are increasingly putting good management to the forefront of their training and development statements and activities, and leadership features increasingly in professional development programmes. As long ago as 1970, the Council of the American Library Association adopted a policy statement on library education and personnel utilization. In this document are listed categories of library personnel, along with the nature of responsibility held by those in each category.

It is interesting to note particularly what is said about professional responsibilities, i.e. that they include 'those of management, which requires independent judgement, interpretation of rules and procedures, analysis of library problems- and formulation of original and creative solutions for solving them'. The skills and knowledge required to carry out those responsibilities certainly need to be sought and developed by the individual, but will prove of immense benefit to the library or information department in which they are employed, as well as to the employing organization at large. Thomas Wilding in discussing career and staff development, says that 'when a library takes inventory of its resources, it needs to measure the abilities and skills of its staff as a major asset'. He goes on to say that 'an effective staff development program will broaden the talent and skills base of the staff, providing the library with greater potential for the accomplishment of its goals'. This is yet another indication of the importance to individual library or information managers of developing corporate awareness so that they can themselves pursue, as well as set up for their staff, appropriate training and development activities relevant to the organization's needs.

The Special Libraries Association (SLA) of the USA has been emphasizing the importance of and promoting the effective development and use of management skills to their members for many years, constantly changing the focus to meet current needs and to enable managers to deal with changes of all kinds. In particular, the need for strong and effective leadership is receiving increasing attention from both individuals and associations.

A quick glance at the programme for the SLA's 1992 conference reveals both formal papers and personal development sessions on the subject. Over recent years the SLA's journal Special libraries has included a number of articles underlining leadership as the key both to the successful running of library and information services and to the future of the LIS profession at large. In one of these Susan DiMattia, in reviewing management literature on the subject of leadership, found a number of ideas which could have been articulated with the LIS profession in mind, particularly those relating to the power of information.

It is suggested that as organizations cannot develop strategies to take themselves forward without having the appropriate knowledge, information professionals could, if they worked at it, take on leading strategic roles within their organizations.

Elizabeth Orna, in looking at the way in which the flow of information is used and managed within organizations, also suggests a link between the power of information and the need for leadership. She sees the role of the information professional as crucial to the development of organizational information policies, thereby identifying another area in which leadership skills would be essential. Leadership is not just about taking your own department, staff and service forward: it also involves stepping outside your particular specialist function and taking an organizational stance; putting forward ideas backed by ways in which they might be implemented for the benefit of the whole organization; acting as a catalyst.

The principal objective of the Australian Information Management Association (AIMA) as listed in its Information Brochure is 'to improve the standard of library management in Australia'. The AIMA puts considerable emphasis on training events and its 1992 list of programmes includes 4 days on leadership effectiveness which centres on the work of the long-established management author Warren Bennis. Each day covers different aspects of management which together provide the skills required for effective leadership. These are outlined below:

- Management of attention - vision, focus, agenda setting and futures
- Management of meaning - internal and external development implications; political, social and economic applications
- Management of trust - values clarification, team building, empowerment, communication
- Management of self - self-assessment and development, personal and organizational action plans

Another related AIMA course looks at the management of organizational change and risk taking, while self-management is additionally dealt with in a separate 2-day workshop.

Why the emphasis on leadership? Because managing is not just about organization and administration, it involves that key resource - people. Leadership is about team building, motivating, encouraging and inspiring your staff, innovating, taking the library/information service forward. It also involves using your skills to play a leading role within the organization as a whole, as well as within the department.

Among the numerous works on leadership, there are several practical guides to help you improve your skills in this area. *Learning to lead* was written with just that aim in mind; it is very readable and contains a number of practical exercises and case studies which could be applied to a range of different management settings. Another practical guide is *Positive leadership : how to build a winning team*, which could act as a useful model for many types of organization.

Continuing to Develop

The above discussion has indicated the breadth of skills aid understanding needed by today's library or information manager. This has also been clearly illustrated in the case studies and examples given. In particular, the two checklists suggested for use in Sections 4 and 5 of the Glasgow Employee Assessment and Development Scheme provide a useful summary of those attributes which help staff to perform well.

The acquisition of wide-ranging management skills is recognized as being essential in a variety of different types of LIS settings and in many countries. In 1989 Rannveig Egerdal Eidet commented on the beginning of a noticeable trend in Norwegian public libraries, and says that 'matters connected with organization and management have been pushed to the top of the agenda within the national public library system'.

He goes on to describe the major management development programme which was at that .time being introduced for chief municipal librarians which he says 'aims to enhance the competence of chief librarians—both as leaders of personnel and as leaders within municipal administrative systems'. He points out certain aspects of the public library system which require specific management treatment. For example, he notes that most libraries have few staff and short opening hours, which means that service to the public has to go before planning and more goal-oriented activities. Other priorities can then suffer as a result.

Jean Michel's interesting paper on LIS education and training in France notes the importance of continuing education to ensure the updating of knowledge and know-how of French professionals. He also sets out reasons for changes in both initial and continuing education which he suggests have become necessary through increased international competition and market globalization; a Europe without frontiers, the 'intelligence revolution', and information and communication technologies. He also puts forward a new typology of professional qualifications and functions. These ideas together provide the basis for an US education and training model crossing sectors, subjects and national boundaries.

Continuing professional development (CPD) is essential for individuals at all levels if service objectives are to be met. CPD is just as necessary for the library assistant without professional qualifications as for the qualified and experienced senior LIS practitioner. Cruz and Santos point to the need for appropriate training for non-graduate assistants in libraries and documentation centres in Portugal, and describe the efforts made by the professional associations there to establish courses of this kind.

Working to professional standards is as important to the employer as it is to the individual practitioner. The Best practice report noted that internal and external issues affecting employing organizations were viewed by LIS staff as identifying areas for their own CPD. This often leads to LIS staff seeking their CPD in subjects outside the LIS field, for example in community subjects, as was discovered by Pors in his research into employment patterns in Denmark. This was also the case in several Australian business libraries.

Studying for a higher degree, within or outside the LIS field, research, writing, lecturing and conducting training all offer considerable opportunity for CPD. Involvement in a variety of professional activities, e.g. participation in subject interest groups, can bring personal development through interaction with other practitioners, stimulating fresh ideas and providing new perspectives.

CPD refers to a range of activities aimed at developing and enhancing knowledge, skills and attitudes. It prepares the individual to carry out their job in the most effective way, increasing motivation and contributing to their long-term progress and achievement. In the hands of an effective manager CPD will ensure not only that manager's personal development, but also that of all their staff, as well as the long-term development and success of the service.

Efficiency, effectiveness, flexibility and managing change all form part of an area of increasing interest to LIS managers, and to their employing organizations, namely, the concept of quality assurance. This important area needs to become an integral part of providing any type of library and information service, kept at the forefront of the minds of all those involved, but particularly the manager. He or she will have responsibility for setting up mechanisms whereby quality in an LIS context can be defined and discussed, with full staff involvement, and monitoring procedures put into place to ensure that quality of service is consistent and of a high standard. Quality is as dependent on the human resource element of library and information provision as it is on the information itself and its supporting systems.

Therefore, staff attitudes and skills form an essential part of quality as perceived by the users of the service, calling for considerable leadership from the manager if a policy of quality assurance is to be successfully implemented. As illustrated by the Aston case study which follows, quality-related LIS activities are likely to be part of an overall organizational strategic plan, which includes a policy of quality assurance, so it is essential that the manager consults with appropriate contacts in the organization to ensure that a coherent approach is taken. However, in addition to quality of service it is equally important for the manager to seek quality in all forms of training and development. In 1988 the Council of the American Library Association adopted guidelines put forward by the Continuing Education Subcommittee of its Standing Committee on Library Education (SCOLE). These set out a comprehensive list of criteria by which to assess the quality of different types of continuing education programmes and activities, and are well worth careful consideration.

An interesting example of the introduction of a quality assurance programme into a special library is described by Anne M. Fredenberg in her capacity as Director of the Kubie Medical Library at the Sheppard and Enoch Pratt Hospital in Baltimore, Maryland, USA. In her article, Fredenberg also offers ten helpful suggestions for managers who may be about to start out on the process of establishing a quality assurance programme for their library or information department.

The library's move towards quality assurance (QA) was part of an institution-wide programme which required departmental managers to spend 1 year developing guidelines and becoming familiar with the systematic methods and record-keeping involved. Fredenberg describes the administrative focus as being on the process, which includes setting goals, analysing current activities, identifying problems, setting priorities, implementing changes, periodic evaluation, and consultation with administration, all of which suggest a number of areas in which the manager may need to develop or improve certain groups of skills such as communication, planning and leadership.

Performance indicators have a valuable part to play in the overall assessment of service quality, as was found at Aston University in the UK. Christine Abbott, who managed the project, talked to me about it, and in particular its implications for US management development.

CASE STUDY: PERFORMANCE INDICATORS IN ASTON UNIVERSITY'S LIBRARY AND INFORMATION SERVICES

The project came about initially as an immediate response to a call from senior management to all departments of the university for increased efficiency and effectiveness. This was in the wake of a radical and comprehensive restructuring aimed at positioning the university as a leading technological institution and centre of excellence. Christine noted that, although performance indicators were introduced in many academic libraries in response to national directives and cost-cutting exercises, at Aston the main interest was not primarily that of justifying resources but of developing improved management tools.

Whilst realising that performance indicators on their own would not constitute better management, they were seen as having considerable potential in terms of improving the quality of management and decision making by providing managers at all levels with the information they needed to make decisions. This particular project was therefore seen as part of a broader exercise of organizational planning, aimed at achieving change to realign the Library and Information Services (LIS) with the new objectives of the university.

High-quality management and skilful financial planning, alongside strong leadership, were essential, and the whole project was underpinned by quantitative systems of assessment to ensure efficiency and effectiveness. At the senior university level a management development programme was adopted to improve and develop appropriate expertise to make sure that the skills necessary to the success of the project were in place. At the start of the project in LIS it was essential to establish just where the performance indicators stood in the planning process, and quite a lot of time was spent in identifying the focus of such a planning strategy. Given that the LIS plan was part of a larger overall strategy, it was essential that performance indicators were seen in relation to both departmental and organizational medium- and long-term objectives. In terms of the LIS objectives, performance indicators had to be viewed as an integrated part of staff development, service provision and customer care.

Christine states the four major objectives of the project as being:

- To develop a series of performance indicators to be used as management tools at all levels
- To explore ways of obtaining better management information from the GEAC computer system
- To review and revise LIS operational statistics
- To develop unit and service costings, primarily as efficiency indicators for use in resource planning and comparative analysis between libraries, and to assist in the university-wide process of bidding for student numbers.

Although the concept of performance indicators was a relatively new one to most of the library staff, a number of measures had already been taken which helped staff to view this as a natural and positive development. A range of development activities and projects under way meant that staff were already involved in activities designed to give the more proactive and service-oriented approach being sought. A university-wide training programme was also developing a corporate culture based on customer care, and this had been enthusiastically adopted by the library staff.

A crucial first step, which proved a very wise one, was to appoint on to the staff a full-time Planning Assistant, rather than rely on the services of an external consultant.

This had a major impact on the way in which the project was viewed by LIS staff, that is, they were able to build a positive relationship with someone who was very much part of the team. For example, the Planning Assistant took turns, along with all the library professionals, to staff the Information Point (Enquiries Desk). As well as providing her with valuable insights into customer needs and the LIS service focus, this move helped her to be seen as a fully integrated member of LIS staff, sharing the professional responsibilities of her colleagues.

It was seen as most important to have full staff involvement and support, as without it the project would be likely to founder and not bring the hoped-for long-term benefits to the LIS, or ultimately to the university. In this, the Planning Assistant acted as a catalyst for change, encouraging managers to consider alternative approaches to problem-solving while at the same time not imposing any particular solutions. Seminars and workshops were organized in which the Planning Assistant as facilitator aimed to focus the staff on current problems and issues. Performance indicators were presented as a means of informing decisions on how to tackle management problems.

A 'bottom up' approach was adopted whereby solutions to managers' individual concerns were sought within the process as it developed, rather than imposing perhaps less precise solutions by working downwards from an all-embracing scheme. By first agreeing a common purpose, the staff themselves were encouraged to put forward suggestions, ideas for improvements, and the performance indicators relevant to their areas of work.

Specific targets were not imposed from outside, but emerged through the process of determining and operating the performance indicators. Two particular areas in which performance indicators were introduced were (a) the cataloguing throughput, and (b) the interlibrary loan service. Both brought to light the fact that procedural changes and more flexible managerial decisions were needed to ensure the efficiency and effectiveness of these services. Staff were encouraged to use office automation skills to produce spreadsheets for maximum analysis of the data, and computer graphics for informative presentation, for example the calculation of delays occurring at each stage of an activity, the production of a series of graphs. Priorities were established for different activities, for example which items should be catalogued first; targets were set based on the analysis of current performance and future possibilities, e.g. acceptable delivery times for interlibrary loans.

APPROACH TO DEVELOPING AND USING PIS

1. Establish objective(s) for the service
2. Analyse the activities involved
3. Compile and cost inputs
4. Summarise outputs
5. Devise an overall PI, or set of Pis
6. Decide the major operational statistics needed
7. Decide what external, supporting data is needed to put the Pis into context
8. Collect PI information
9. Analyse findings
10. Compare findings with objectives
11. Take remedial action if/when necessary better to achieve the objective and/or optimise the 3 Es.*
12. Monitor the effects of remedial action on the Pis

Fig. 1 : Approach to developing and using Pis

*Economy, efficiency, effectiveness

Key management points that arose out of the project as a whole were:

- The central role performance indicators can play in the staff development process
- The importance of systematic management of information gathered during such a project and above all
- The interrelated nature of different areas of service.

Following the initial project, the use of performance indicators in the LIS at Aston is now seen as part of a wider activity of operational planning, as a tool in the quest for Total Quality Management. One clear message that has come out of the project is that knowing how to use performance indicators is just part of the portfolio of skills needed by today's LIS manager in applying such techniques. Many other skills relating to qualitative as well as quantitative aspects of their use are required.

The use of performance indicators in a different sort of library is described in a helpful booklet published by Hertfordshire County Council's Schools Library Service. Although produced as a set of guidelines for use in secondary schools, the definitions and checklists it provides make it very useful to any LIS manager seeking to introduce the concept. Extracts from the booklet are reproduced below:

How to use Performance Indicators

They can be used:

- by the librarian for the review and development programme
- as a checklist to assess the current state of provision to ascertain what can be developed quickly and economically
- to identify contacts to be made
- to highlight areas for long-term improvement

- for annual assessment to evaluate progress made over the previous twelve months
- to collate results for an annual report to the Senior Management Team of the School; Governors and Parent Teachers Association
- to assist in future planning, development and spending

Target Statements for the Library

The target statements are linked directly to the aims and specific objectives for development and are in no particular order.

Accommodation and Ambience

- There is an attractive working environment.

Access

- The library is open before, during and after the school day to all staff and students.

Guiding

- This should facilitate easy use of the library, and be accurate, clear and professional looking.

Stock

- Appropriate and accurate stock in good condition covering the school's curriculum and recreational needs.

Staffing

- The library is professionally staffed on a full-time basis with clerical support. This will enable students and staff to make maximum use of the resources and information.

Funding

- To maintain and improve the school library in terms of space, furniture, materials and equipment.

Service Provision and Planning

- The school is aware of and exploits all available external agencies as appropriate.

Information Technology

- There are computers in the library used for a variety of purposes.

Policy

- A written policy exists, is agreed and is regularly reviewed.

Promotion

- Active promotion of the library and its resources to all staff and students occurs.

Information skills

- An agreed information skills policy exists, and is reviewed in line with curricular need.

Cross Phase Liaison

- Awareness of the current information skills practised in feeder primary schools and knowledge of the skills required for students' future needs. This ensures a progressive approach to life skills.

Monitoring and Evaluation

- Library performance is systematically evaluated to ensure effective delivery and potential.

[The booklet then continues by setting out a number of detailed criteria under each heading, beside which there are two columns headed OPTIMUM and MINIMUM under which the stage of achievement of each criterion is noted. This will provide a detailed overall plan and indicate where most resourcing and effort will be required to ensure that targets are met. It will also indicate the line for future planning.]

(Reproduced from *If you can't measure it, you can't manage it: performance indicators for secondary schools* [3] by kind permission of Hertfordshire County Council's Schools Library Service.)

The performance being assessed may be that of the individual, the service or the organization as a whole. Each will have an impact on the other areas being assessed. Good management practice involves the constant review of all aspects of the service to ensure not only that objectives are being met, but that the objectives themselves continue to be relevant. If not, they too may need to be modified, one of the suggestions in the CSIRO case study which follows.

CASE STUDY : CSIRO

CSIRO (Commonwealth Scientific and Industrial Research Organization) is Australia's foremost scientific research and development enterprise in terms of the scale, diversity and quality of its research activities, and because of the consequent benefit to Australia of those activities. CSIRO's main role is to conduct strategic research to develop technologies for all sectors of Australian industry; to improve the management of Australia's natural resources; to protect Australia's unique environment; and to promote the well-being of the Australian people.

In corporate sector terms, CSIRO is a conglomerate of 32 individual 'companies' organized into 6 major industry-oriented groups. It has a total staff of about 7000 spread across Australia. CSIRO's role in Australian research and development is particularly significant because it undertakes a large proportion of government-funded R & D, and consequently, a large proportion of all R & D in Australia. CSIRO's Information Services Unit coordinates and supports a network of regional site libraries and is heavily involved in database development, as well as carrying out a range of other LIS activities, including the organization of a considerable collection of scientific material. LIS staff, along with all other departments, participate in the organization's Performance Planning and Evaluation scheme, introduced in 1991. The scheme was publicized to staff through a series of meetings at every site and by the circulation of the following article in the staff newsletter:

PERFORMANCE PLANNING AND EVALUATION; the wheels of progress and how to ride them.

A new method of assessing the work of CSIRO staff members comes into force on July 1 this year - Performance Planning and Evaluation, or PPE, to its friends. Below is a brief account - based on information supplied by the Human Resources Branch - designed to give CoResearch readers a glimpse of what's in store.

The CSIRO's new Performance Planning and Evaluation program aims at top quality work, including leadership, linked to improved career planning and development. The system will follow a yearly cycle, with the appraisal period beginning in May and winding up in June the following year. Here's how it goes.

Stage 1 - setting the performance objectives and development plan

You begin by listing your job responsibilities on the PPE form and giving it to your manager. The two of you then get together for a formal planning discussion with specific tasks:

- Working out a personal development plan.

This is to give you and your manager a basis for career planning and development activities. You simply write down your career preferences and your development and training priorities.

- Clarifying work activities and responsibilities.

You do this by writing down your broad functions, your work activities, and your areas of responsibility within your programme. These will, of course, be related to the programme objectives, so this is the time to clarify these with your manager.

- Setting work objectives

This is to make sure you and your manager have the same idea about exactly what work you are to get done during the appraisal period, and how that work will be evaluated. That is, which activities are the key ones on which your performance will be judged; your work objectives should be specific about both the quantity and the quality of the results expected from you in key areas of the job.

- Recording your 'competencies'

This simply means copying in the 'competencies' that are listed as expected at your classification level. The question of whether they actually match your real skills doesn't arise until assessment time. Competencies are still something of a mystery to most staff at CSIRO, but you will have them in time for your first PPE sessions. In the meantime they could be roughly described as combinations of skill, knowledge and aptitude, as opposed to qualifications. Problem-solving ability, for example, will be one of them, and a CSOF 2 would be expected to have a lower level of that ability, or competency, than a CSOF 3. They will be an important part of your assessment for promotion, and CoResearch will carry an article soon on this part of the new system.

You can take a colleague into this first formal session if you feel uncertain about handling it on your own. When you and your manager have agreed on all this and written it down, both of you sign the form and it is sent off to the next level up, that is, to your manager's manager. With approval at that level, you and your manner can also set down extra training or resources you feel you need to achieve your work objectives.

It's not set in concrete, however. The work objectives and the personal development plan can both be modified during the appraisal period, though all such modifications should be endorsed by the higher level manager. And that higher level manager is also the one who steps in to mediate if you and your manager disagree on what you should write into your PPE agreement at that first meeting.

Stage 2 - continuing performance review and feedback

This stage goes on for the whole evaluation period, that is all year. The point of it is to make sure that managers have frequent communication with staff members. Your manager should provide you with continuous feedback, monitoring your progress and giving you the encouragement and support you need to achieve your objectives and improve your skills. You and your manager should both keep a 'significant events diary' to try to make sure neither of you falls into the trap of remembering only what you want to remember or forgetting things that happened a long time ago. It's all too easy to let this week's triumph or disaster overshadow the rest of the year's work.

Stage 3 - completing the appraisal

Like Stage 1, this stage is a meeting between you and your manager, and again, you can have a fellow worker with you if you want to. If the manager has been doing his or her job there shouldn't be any surprises at this meeting, since you'll have been getting continuous feedback on whether your work was satisfactory or not. You should prepare for the meeting simply by summarizing your achievements over the year.

This formal appraisal discussion focuses on a comparison of your achievements and performance with the objectives and competencies you wrote down at the first meeting, or as modified by both of you during the year. There may also be important achievements that are not on that original agreement but should be considered nevertheless.

Your manager should prepare for the discussion by:

- looking back over the achievements noted in the significant events diary;
- if necessary, seeking relevant information from other sources; and
- trying to anticipate what concerns you might want to bring up about your career development and what planned activities for the unit might affect your next appraisal cycle.

By the end of the meeting the two of you should have been able to agree on your overall performance, and this agreement should include an assessment of:

- your achievements, including any special circumstance that affected whether or not, or how well, you managed your agreed work objectives;
- the level of competencies you showed; and
- your development during the period, identifying strengths and/or weaknesses, especially with an eye to your development needs, which can then be incorporated into the personal development plan you prepare at the beginning of the next appraisal cycle.

When you have agreed on all this, your manager will summarize your overall level of performance as 'very good', 'satisfactory', 'fair', or 'deficient'. If appropriate, he or she can then recommend merit awards and, if authorized, approve incremental advancement. With this system increments are no longer automatic, and if your performance is 'fair' or 'deficient' your pay will not rise. But, on the plus side, your manager can reward good performance with any or all of the following:

- accelerated advancement - this will be considered where your work for this year and other years seems to be consistently outstanding;
- incentive payment - where your current year's work seems outstanding; and
- reclassification - where your achievements and competencies seem to justify a higher level.

Whether or not you get an increment will depend on whether or not you have achieved your work objectives and competencies. In some cases, however, your manager may decide that your performance was satisfactory even though you didn't achieve your objectives, judging that the fault lay in circumstances beyond your control, for example, a bushfire may have burned out your experimental plantings, your computer may have broken down repeatedly, or you may have had an unusual amount of time off with sickness. Or, as often happens, the task you were working on may have opened up like a flower, revealing undreamt-of complexities.

In all of this, if you and your manager don't see eye to eye, you move to the next-up manager.

Confidentiality

Your manager will keep your form handy, so that you can have access to it whenever you like, but will not let others see it. You, of course, can keep a copy for your own reference.

As each appraisal cycle is completed your form will go onto a confidential file, with access allowed only to those with a legitimate right, as verified by the Divisional

Personnel Officer or equivalent. (In practice, that would normally be appropriate Divisional personnel staff and appropriate management staff.)

The next cycle

The next cycle begins as soon as the old one is complete, but you might like to take a few days to think about work objectives for the next period, and that's fine. You and your manager would then arrange a good time for another Stage 1 meeting, beginning the process for the next appraisal period.

The information contained in the above article was presented as a leaflet which was circulated to CSIRO staff. The leaflet also set out the three stages of the process as a diagram, showing their relationship to other personnel processes. This provides a very useful example of one of the ways in which management can communicate information in a clear and easy-to-follow format.

STAFF DEVELOPMENT TRAINING: PROBLEMS AND SOLUTIONS

The evidence is all around us that individual performance management, in the form of performance goals and goal-based self-assessment, is ever more widely acknowledged to be a key tool in library management. The surge of recent interest in strategic planning has placed new emphasis on the development of organizational goals and goal-based evaluation systems. The quality management movement has shifted the emphasis away from some of the more rigid aspects of management-by-objectives (*e.g.*, quotas) toward the view that goals and goal-based self-assessment are a creative and flexible means of continual quality improvement. And the shift toward self-managing work groups and other highly participatory models in some of our libraries has suggested a strong need for individual and small-unit performance planning through the use of goals and objectives: if work groups and the individuals in them are to manage themselves effectively, they need the tools to do so.

While they typically acknowledge the importance of such performance planning, organizations are nonetheless faced with significant problems of training and orientation when they decide to require performance objectives and meaningful self-assessment of staff. This article describes what one academic research library, the University of California at San Diego (UCSD), is doing to train staff in performance management skills.

Background

Until the late 1980's, goals and objectives had been only an informal part of the performance review process for librarians at UCSD. Though self-reviews of librarians occasionally mentioned goals and objectives, in reality they were often ignored as part of the process. Moreover, written self-reviews, a key part of the review package, typically took the form of unevaluated lists of activities rather than carefully assessed accomplishments that were explicitly related to organizational goals.

Three developments within the last few years have led to an intensification of the goal-based self-evaluation process throughout the library:

1. A new University Librarian stipulated that performance reviews for librarians be goal-based and that statements of goals become a formal part of the evaluation process. Goals and objectives, formerly discussed on an informal basis between supervisor and librarian, were now to be part of the official review file as well. An important parallel expectation was that goal-based reviews would be truly evaluative-in their self-reviews, reviewers were expected to focus on measurable accomplishments, on the value of those accomplishments to the Library

and its users, and on both the strengths and areas needing improvement in their performances. Though these may seem innocuous changes on their face, the implications for accountability were significant, and so a generous period of transition to the new system was provided.

2. The Library developed a comprehensive Strategic Plan, The Library Without Walls, with a hierarchy of mission, goals, objectives, and action plans. The clear message was that departments and individual staff were to look to the Strategic Plan for guidance in developing their own goals and objectives, which would further the goals of the Plan.

3. Through a change in University personnel policy, non-librarian professionals (for example, technical and management staff in the Systems Office, the Library Business Office, and processing departments) were required to develop goals and objectives each year and to relate annual performance evaluations to goals.

Suddenly, like it or not, some ninety professional staff, both librarians and non-librarians, were responsible for developing performance goals and objectives, relating them to the goals of the Library and their departments, and measuring their performance against those goals.

As with any significant organizational change, some anxiety resulted and a number of concerns were expressed. There was concern that goals which were perfectly reasonable at the beginning of the year might be superseded by goals related to new program development, the need to work on urgent projects such as journal cancellations, or any one of the myriad problems that one simply cannot plan for in a large, dynamic organization. Staff wondered if there would be penalties if all performance goals were not achieved. What about the ongoing aspects of performance-daily service at a reference desk, original cataloging, materials selection?

Wouldn't it be difficult to construct goals for these "routine" activities that were an everyday part of one's core job? On a more practical level, some staff were simply less comfortable than others with the rhetorical challenges-the writing tasks-represented by the new expectations, especially the potential discomfort of suggesting in a formal written document that there might be areas for self-improvement.

The burden of interpreting these changes and training staff in related new skills fell on the supervisors, who had always been-and remain-key actors in the performance review "partnership." To help both supervisors and reviewees with these important new tasks, the Library has developed two training tools: a half-day workshop in goals and objectives and a model goal-based self-review that suggests but does not impose a framework for the process.

The workshop developed out of a request from librarians that training in the goals and objectives piece of the process was needed. Late in 1990, Susan Jurow of the Office of Management Services, Association of Research Libraries, after several consultation sessions with Library Administration, offered a day-and-a-half workshop for all UCSD librarians, including administrators. In 1991, the author conducted three follow-up events for staff who had not attended the 1990 workshop: (1) a brief session for librarians early in the year; (2) a five-hour workshop for non-librarian professionals around the same time; (3) a joint half-day workshop for both librarians and non-librarian professionals during the fall. It is the latter workshop, adapted from the original Jurow design, that has become the continuing annual training event for new professionals. It is offered each fall just before performance reviews begin.

As a parallel training effort, even before the workshops were offered, the author had developed a fictitious goal-based self-review to illustrate what he had in mind when he thought about such a document. Though originally intended only for those in his reporting line, this model has been made available to most other professionals in the Library.

These training efforts were meant to achieve several purposes:

1. to demystify the performance goal-setting and self evaluation processes;
2. to promote the view that planning with goals and objectives could enhance individual performance effectiveness;
3. to relate the performance goals process to organizational goals and organizational effectiveness;
4. to save professionals time as they perform this annual task.

The Workshop

The workshop is scheduled to run from 10:00 a.m. to 3:30 p.m., with an hour for lunch. It is held on campus but away from the library to intensify focus on the task at hand. After a review of the objectives of the workshop and the agenda for the day, participants are asked to consider three key questions:

1. What is a goal?
2. What do you like/value about the goals process?
3. What do you dislike about the process?

The resulting census is reported on flip chart sheets. This exercise, especially the like/dislike section, gets issues and problems out for discussion as soon as possible, enabling participants to articulate both positive and negative feelings while at the same time having their responses become merged in the total group response.

Next, a conceptual framework for performance planning is provided. *Planning* is a classic managerial responsibility;

developing goals and objectives is, furthermore, a key activity in planning. The organizational context is presented: the Strategic Plan, the goal focus of Library planning, and the requirements of the performance review process for all library professionals.

The benefits of goals and objectives in an organizational setting are then enumerated:

1. Goals clarify where we want to go so that we understand better how to get there.
2. They decode expectations for all to see and understand;
3. They establish a foundation on which to build improvement;
4. They help us coordinate our activities with other departments, staff;
5. They help us distribute work and effort more equitably.

Next, goals and objectives are related to performance measures, a key concept in the remainder of the training. Four types of measures commonly applied to staff performance are described;

1. Effort, which describes inputs (example: 43 person/ hours of planning time);
2. Process, which describes activities curried out (example: three meetings, one conference call, and a final report);
3. Performance, which describes the results of effort (ex- ample: on line search service established);
4. Outcomes, which describe final effects (example: better service to users).

Effort and process are often used as measures of performance because they are easiest to capture. *Performance* and *outcomes* are more difficult to measure and are thus often slighted in the goal-setting and self-evaluation process, but they are, in fact, more indicative of actual useful accomplishment. In constructing performance goals, though all kinds of measurable goals are possible and even useful, the most useful are those that point us toward *performance* and *outcomes.* Throughout the rest of the training, participants are pushed to develop goals that can be measured in these ways.

The focus on measurable results provides the framework for the next exercise. Here the participants gain some practice in converting "raw" work activity into measurable results. A few examples are offered to get them started on a group exercise:

Activity	Measurable Results
1. Fundraising	a. number of dollars raised
	b. number of contacts made with potential donors
	c. improved grant-writing skill as measured by peer judgement
2. Working the reference desk	a. number of questions answered successfully
	b. improved reference interview skills as measured by user satisfaction survey

Participants are then given a chance to work together in small groups practicing the shift from work activity to measurable result. Their work is reviewed and discussed by the entire group.

Now the group is ready to work on goals and objectives. First, three basic kinds of performance goals are enumerated:

1. *Organizational Goals*. These directly further the work of the organization. Examples: to develop a new service for library users; to improve an existing service; to change a processing procedure to improve both efficiency and accuracy.

2. *Performance Effectiveness Goals*. These are instrumental goals related to the manner in which staff carry out their work. Such goals might relate to: time management, delegation, communication effectiveness, ability to plan and organize, training skills, effective relations with colleagues.

3. *Professional Goals*. These describe how the employee intends to make a contribution to his or her profession, as appropriate, through such means as presentation and publication.

Next, the criteria for effective performance goals are reviewed:

1. Goals should suggest *movement* from a present state to a desired state; use of words such as *enhance, improve, further*, and *increase* denote such movement.

2. They should be *measurable*, preferably in quantitative terms. Some goals are best stated in qualitative terms: even these can be measured, for example, by seeking feedback through surveys and comments from other staff.

3. They should, whenever possible, *reflect organizational goals* and should clearly be seen as advancing its mission.

4. They should be *challenging but achievable*. When one sets too many goals or unachievable goals, frustration results.

5. They should be *ranked in importance* if possible. Part of performance planning is determining priorities.

6. They should be *dynamic and adaptable to change*, especially if circumstances change significantly. Target dates should be included, if possible, as an aid to setting priorities and allocating time.

7. They should be *reviewed and renegotiated regularly*. Such an approach provides both a periodic check on progress and a safety valve in case a goal turns out to be impossible to achieve.

8. They should be *focused*. A key question for the staff member is, what are you working on in your performance? A focused goal-based plan might include: (a) two or three major projects, (b) development of one or two new skills or knowledge areas, and (c) work on one or two performance dimensions (example: time management). It is not necessary to develop goals to cover every area of one's position description-such an approach can in fact lead to a feeling of being overwhelmed and frustrated.

9. They should, if possible, indicate an *ultimate aim*. In a service organization like an academic research library, such an aim would, of course, be service.

Participants are then given an opportunity to convert the material already generated (job activities and measurable results) into goals and objectives. This work is also done in small groups. Problems and issues arising in this exercise are discussed in the larger group.

The final exercise of the afternoon is a "goals clinic." Participants are asked to provide the trainer ahead of time with some of their previously written goals and objectives; they are asked particularly to submit goals that they have had problems writing. The trainer rewrites these slightly to protect anonymity, but the basic form is left intact. The entire group then gets a chance to critique these "masked" goals, using the principles learned through the experiences of the previous few hours. Participants are thus engaged in the process of creating specific, measurable goals at several junctures throughout the workshop.

The Model Self-review : Luis Libros

The other training device used is a written model-a fictitious self-review by a librarian named Luis Libros, who works at a fictitious UC campus. The model is intended not only to illustrate effective performance goals and objectives but also what a performance review based on those goals and objectives might look like as well. Three performance review issues are illustrated:

(1) that the self-review focus on accomplishments',
(2) that it be truly evaluative, not merely descriptive and enumerative; and
(3) that both strengths and areas to work on in the performance be cited. Here is an excerpt from this self-review:

Goal #l. Improve my skills in mediated on-line searching.

Objective: Attend tutorial on new [psychology] database to be offered on campus, 1990.

Objective: Take on a larger share of departmental searching load; increase load by 50% to 15 searches per week by January 1991.

Accomplishments: As a relatively new librarian in the Ed/Psych Library, I needed to enhance basic skills. I was comfortable searching only 9 databases at the beginning of the period, and per session searching time was too long. The tutorial turned out to be a marketing strategy by the publisher, but it did serve to outline the basic structure of the database, which I have searched several times since. Doing more searches was a useful approach-a powerful motivator for me. I have been doing 13-16 searches per week.

Evaluation of accomplishments: On-line time has decreased by 28% on the average, and my "scores" on user evaluation forms have gone from an average of 7.1 to an average of 9.2. I can now search 22 data bases with ease and 15 others with occasional references to the manuals.

Areas to work on: For the time being, my department head and I are satisfied with my progress and believe that more practice is the key to further enhancement of skills and greater user satisfaction.

Goal #2. Enhance contribution to the orientation/ instruction program for new graduate students in Education.

Objective: Redesign two-hour orientation session by June 1990 so that newly designed sessions can be offered September 1990.

Objective: Develop one-hour sessions on ERIC, PSYCH-LIT, and DISSABS for new masters students by October 1991.

Objective: Develop twelve special screens on Curriculum Collection for hypercard orientation installation by February 1990.

Accomplishments: The two-hour orientation session redesign was completed and new sessions offered as planned. Only the ERIC session was developed and tested. It was found that most students do not attend structured sessions on searching end-user databases, so we focused on point-of-use instruction instead. Responsibility for the hypercard screens was given to another librarian.

Evaluation of accomplishments: Pro- and post-testing of students indicate preliminarily that the two-hour orientation sessions are more effective than our previous three-hour sessions in communicating basic information about the library. I have gathered from site interviews that the point-of-use handbook I developed on PSYCH- LIT has been very popular and effective in helping students get the most out of their searching. I am working on a similar handbook for ERIC. I had more enthusiasm than skill for the hypercard project and am glad that my department head suggested it be reassigned.

Areas to work on: Instructional design is an area of strength for me, and I would like to make it even stronger by taking two relevant courses in the School of Education during the next review period. At the same time, the hypercard experience taught me that I need to acquire basic skills in the use of computers in teaching and reduce my apprehension about it as well.

All of the training objectives for the model self-review are illustrated in this excerpt. The objectives are specific and measurable. The focus is on results and outcomes rather than on effort and process. Accomplishments are really evaluated and areas to work on are candidly appraised. Though the outline is very structured, it allows a certain flexibility, even informality, of expression. In presenting the model to the staff, we have encouraged them to use it or not, as they choose, but the expectation remains that the key elements of specificity, measurability, focus on accomplishments, and true evaluation of both strengths and areas to work on be present.

Evaluation of Results

Though no formal evaluation of these training tools has taken place, anecdotal reports of improvement in the quality of self-re-views and the goals and objectives on which they are based suggest some positive results. Of course, the benefits of supervisorial attention to these new expectations and the fact that reviewees have now gained more practice are significant factors as well. Nonetheless, informal comments solicited in preparation of tins article suggest some direct benefits of the training. Many participants found the first day-and-a-half workshop useful not only for its content but also because the presence of administrators, participating throughout the event, enabled the group to address issues of organizational culture. About this and the later workshops, participants responded:

1. that such an approach promotes shared values and brings consistency of practice throughout the library;
2. that talking about the problems, the issues, and the writing tasks with colleagues-knowing co-workers have the same anxieties-made the process go easier; some participants have continued the process of helping one another with goal for- mulation;
3. that the workshops presented direct clarification of administrative expectations;
4. that it was helpful to learn that there was more than one way to write effective goals and self-evaluations;
5. that it was useful to receive criticism through the anonymous process of the goals clinic.

Many respondents have found the model self-review useful as well, particularly those engaging in the process for the first time.

1. Again, the model clarified administrative expectations.
2. Even though the format was not always followed exactly, the model provided a clear guide to required ingredients in the self-review and useful suggestions about tone and approach, especially in evaluative sections.
3. Supervisors have found it useful in helping to explain their expectations in the review process.

Finally, some respondents gave clear credit to their supervisors in helping them through the process, with one person citing "the more useful [but also] more painful iterative process of working with my supervisor to define goals and objectives and to make reviews reflect them."

Conclusion

The UCSD experience suggests that taking a training approach to performance management can make a difference in improving the quality of the goal-based self-review process and thus the effectiveness and relevance of organizational planning. Such an approach focuses on the most fundamental behavioral level-the writing skills needed to develop effective performance goals, objectives, and self-reviews-rather than on the more theoretical aspects of the subject. The integration of librarians and professionals who are not librarians in the training, even though their needs are somewhat different, proved successful. Most importantly, this training approach rests on the assumption that individual goal-setting and self-evaluation represent an important direction for our organizations if we are to capitalize on the creativity that results when staff are empowered to manage themselves within a framework of clearly articulated organizational expectations.

4

STAFF DEVELOPMENT : EDUCATIONAL ECOLOGY, STRUCTURE AND PURPOSE

INTRODUCTION

Peter M. Senge opens his book *The Fifth Discipline: The Art & Practice of The Learning Organization* with the following statement:

> *"From a very early age, we are taught to break apart problems, to fragment the world. This apparently makes complex tasks and subjects more manageable, but we pay a hidden, enormous price. We can no longer see the consequences of our actions; we lose our intrinsic sense of connection to a larger whole."*

The profession's literature is filled with articles and editorials about library education and its current lamentable state. These articles tend, however, to break the problem apart and do not examine the profession's educational system. This article examines the library profession's educational ecology and concludes with some recommendations for strengthening this system. This examination consists of four components: an examination of another profession's educational ecology, a summary of three different futures-oriented views of the library profession, a general discussion of the current educational system, and a proposed "Green Movement" for the profession whose purpose is to address the weaknesses that exist in the current educational ecology. This article focuses on the continuing education component of the profession's educational system.

MARK TWAIN'S REMARK ABOUT LIBRARY EDUCATION

A few years ago a colleague was accepted to the School of Law at Duke University. In the packet of information sent from the university was a letter from the School's Dean. In her letter, the dean suggested some readings that new law students might wish to consider as they prepared to enter law school. One of the titles contained in the dean's recommended readings was Mark Twain's *Life on the Mississippi*. This title not only appeared on her suggested reading list, but was strongly recommended. In fact, the dean indicated that if a student was only going to read a single work to prepare for a legal education that work should be Mark Twain's *Life on the Mississippi*. The dean went on to state that she knew of no title that did a better job of describing what a professional education entails.

Life on the Mississippi was published in 1874. It describes how Mark Twain became a river boat pilot. The book opens with a description of the Mississippi River's history, its importance, and its most visible characteristic: its tendency to change. For the middle of America during the mid-1800s, the Mississippi was everything. The livelihood of the entire region depended on the river and the fact that it was navigable. What was true for the region was even more so for an individual.

If a landowner's property bordered the river, he was wealthy. If his land did not border the river, he was not. In Twain's vision, wealth and poverty were determined by the simple fact of whether or not one owned river front property. The Mississippi, however, was constantly changing its course and one's fortune rose or fell according to these changes. Twain gives vivid descriptions about the river's changes and the personal and communal boons and busts that resulted.

After his opening chapters, Twain writes about his becoming a river boat pilot. In order to become a pilot, an individual had to find an experienced pilot who was willing to take on an apprentice or "cub" pilot. In Twain's case, he finds a Mr. Bixby who after much cajoling agrees to accept Twain as a cub. The bulk of Twain's education is spent in the pilot house next to Mr. Bixby "learning the river." In one of his first lessons, Twain learns that he just can't memorize landmarks as a way of knowing where he is on the Mississippi. Instead, he must learn the "shape" of the river because as Bixby points out, the river nul its landmarks not only change but look different at different times. The way a dead oak looks on a bend during the day and the way the same dead oak looks on the same bend on a moonlit night are entirely different and, therefore, deceiving and likewise potentially disastrous. In essence, Twain discovers that, instead of learning the river's specifics, he must learn its dynamics. It is shortly after this particular lesson about the shape of the river that Twain says of his education:

> *Two things seemed pretty apparent to me. One was, that in order to be a pilot a man had to learn more than any one man ought to be allowed to know; and the other was, that he must learn it all over again in a different way every twenty-four hours.*

Twain continues his discussion of his education by describing the community of learning that typified the river pilot profession. Because of the nature of the river, a pilot was constantly learning and relearning the river. This fact is discussed early on in the book when we learn mat pilots who are not currently engaged or whose boats are lying in port usually accompany boats going down river to get a "fresh look" at the river before they begin taking their own boats down river. This was standard practice and a riverboat's pilot house was frequently filled with pilots. During these trips down river the pilots spent most of their time exchanging ideas and information about the river as well as commenting on each other's performance. This community of learning also manifested itself in one final way. The pilots formed an association. One of the main services of this association was the continuing education of its members.

All along the river wharf boxes were posted. All association members had keys to these boxes. Inside the boxes were reports of the conditions of the river. Of this service Twain says:

> *The pilot who deposited a report in the Cairo box (after adding to it the details of every crossing all the way down from St. Louis) took out and read half a dozen fresh reports (from upward bound steamers) concerning the river between Cairo and Memphis, posted himself thoroughly, returned them to the box, and went back aboard his boat again so armed against accident that he could not possibly get his boat into trouble without bringing the most ingenious carelessness to his aid. Imagine the benefits of so admirable a system in a piece of river twelve or thirteen hundred miles long, whose channel was shifting every day! The pilot who had formerly been obliged to put up with seeing a shoal place once or possibly twice a month, had a hundred sharp eyes to watch it for him now, and bushels of intelligent brains to tell him how to run it. His information about it was seldom twenty-four hours old. If the reports in the last box chanced to leave any misgivings on his mind concerning a treacherous crossing, he had his remedy; he blew his steam-whistle in a peculiar way as soon as he saw a boat approaching; the signal was answered in a peculiar way if that boat's pilots were association men; and then the two steamers ranged alongside and all uncertainties were*

swept away by fresh information furnished to the inquirer by word of mouth and in minute detail.'

One of the things Twain does in Life on the Mississippi is give us a glimpse of the educational ecology of the river pilot profession. It is a system focused on preparing individuals to practice this profession. It is a system in which most of the learning is done at the point of practice. It is a system which acknowledges the need for the constant updating of its members' skills and knowledge. It is a profession that provides this updating at the point of practice and in a timely manner. It is also a profession that has established itself as a learning community where future river pilots are educated by experienced pilots at the point of practice and members of the profession assume the dual responsibilities of self-education and the education of their peers. This system is how one profession ensured that it had an ample number of members who were competent and qualified to steer an entire region's wealth through changing, if not troubled, waters.

AS THE CENTURY TURNS : LIBRARIANSHIP IN THE 1990S AND BEYOND

In the 1990s the library profession finds itself in waters that are both changing and troubled. The continued closing of library schools, an increase in the number of schools under review, and concern about the type of individuals who are choosing to enter the profession are some of the many factors that are fueling an increase, in the amount of time and literature devoted to examining the library profession and its role in our society. Three documents which discuss this dilemma are: *Statement on the Decade of the Librarian 1990-2000, Information 2000: Library and Information Services for the 21 st Century, and Strategic Vision for Professional Librarians.*

The *Statement of the Decade of the Librarian 1990-2000* was prepared as part of the American Library Association's strategic planning process. This document, which was approved by ALA Council at the 1991 annual meeting in Atlanta, opens with the following vision statement describing a librarian in the year 2000;

> *The vision of the librarian in year 2000 is as a leader, a fighter, an expert, a partner, a model, and a professional. In order to achieve tins vision we must reposition librarianship as the information profession in society by enhancing society's perception of librarians; each librarian must also take responsibility for his or her own self-image and professional definition: acting as professionals with a mission instead of employees with a job. Library employment; must recognise their responsibility for investing in their personnel.*

This statement goes on to provide six strategic directions tor ensuring that this profile of the librarian is realized. This vision is to be achieved by bringing the best people into the field, educating people for library/information careers, creating a work force that reflects a pluralistic society, compensating librarians at a more competitive level, keeping the librarians we have, and increasing recognition for librarians as information professionals in a changing society. The main focus of these strategies is the recruitment of "new blood" into the profession. In fact, it is only the fifth direction, "keeping the librarians we have," that is targeted at individuals who are currently practicing librarians.

The 1991 White House Conference on Library and Information Services identified three challenges for libraries in the near future. These challenges were in the areas of literacy, productivity, and democracy. The summary report of this conference *Information 2000* contains a complete listing of the conference recommendations and library based solutions to the challenges facing our society in the three areas. The proposed solutions rely heavily on technology or related approaches to the provision of library and information services. The report is filled with requests for federal action, federal funding, partnerships, coalitions, the development of model programs, and the education and training of librarians. In tact, three of the ninety-five recommendations and petitions were directed specifically at personnel and staff development. These were: to study alternative delivery systems for providing access to master's level study; to provide scholarships, grants, and loans at all levels to support continuing education, staff development and training in library and information science; and to increase financial aid to attract minorities to the profession. Here again, two out of three recommendations are geared to initial recruitment to the profession. It should also be pointed out that none of these recommendations was viewed as a high priority by the conference as a whole.

The document which contains the most sweeping recommendations for change in the profession is *Strategic Vision for Professional Librarians*, a statement developed by the Strategic Visions Steering Committee. This committee is composed of a group of library leaders who have been engaged in thoughtful discussion about the profession and its future. They are not affiliated with any organization. This group of concerned librarians, however, has developed a vision of the profession which makes a commitment to selecting and delivering information that users need at the point and moment of need; to educating users to manage information; to furthering the development of the "virtual library," a concept of information housed electronically and deliverable without regard to its location or to time; to taking responsibility for information policy development; and to experimenting with new forms of organizational structure and staffing within libraries to enable delivery of new types of services to users, especially remote users, or users of the growing "virtual library. This document also has several recommendations about recruitment and development of the profession's work force. The following specific recommendations are made:

> *Publicize the unique advantage at which the "information age" places librarians as information professionals.*
>
> *Strengthen the degree-granting programs, develop effective relationships with other information-related disciplines, and establish alternative models for attaining professional credentials.*
>
> *Attract and retain creative and innovative people.*
>
> *Incorporate different competencies/professionals into the emerging information delivery environment.*
>
> *Address the importance of continuing professional education.*

Again, four of the five recommendations deal with the recruitment of new blood or new talent to the field. It is only the last recommendation that addresses the need for the continuing education and development of existing personnel.

While each of these documents identifies different challenges for the profession and proposes somewhat different solutions to these challenges, they concur on two themes: they recognize that librarianship must change if it is to remain a viable and productive part of society; and they rely heavily on "new recruits" to the profession to carry out their proposed changes.

This strategy will not work. There are two compelling reasons why the "new recruit" strategy is doomed to failure. First, there are approximately 150,000 practicing librarians in this country.

This compares to the approximately 4,400 new librarians graduated each year by the ALA-accredited library schools in tills country and Canada. These 4,400 individuals, the "new blood" of the profession, will be hired, oriented, trained, supervised and acculturated to the profession by the 150,000 individuals who are currently members of it. Many of these

150,000 persons will reinforce the status-quo. By the time the "new blood" gets to any position of power or influence it will be virtually indistinguishable from the profession's status quo. Second, Kathleen Heim and William E. Moen surveyed students enrolled in accredited library and information science programs in the spring of 1988. They found that approximately 53% of all students had some library experience and that 34% had held a full-time position in a library.

They also found that for 88% of the 53% that had some library experience, this experience had a positive influence on their decision to become librarians." This means that at least half of the profession's new recruits are already partially acculturated to the profession prior to entering it. In fact, these individuals are choosing librarianship because they have some first-hand knowledge of it and like what they see. These two factors indicate that any new talent that enters the field is going to be exposed to an enormous amount of pressure to conform to existing practices, policies, and standards. Yet, the three documents described earlier all indicate that what is needed is a new vision of the profession that is complete with new practices, policies, and standards.

The repositioning of the library profession will not be achieved by recruiting new talent to the profession. The profession does not need new librarians as much as it needs renewed librarians. The repositioning of the library profession can only be achieved through the continuing education and development of existing staff.

CONTINUING LIBRARY EDUCATION: AN ECOLOGICAL PORTRAIT

The primary mode of continuing education in the library profession is the workshop. The workshop or conference has been indicated as the preferred mode of continuing education in a study of Florida public library directors by McCrossan.

This study asked public library directors in Florida to discuss which modes of professional development or continuing education had been most helpful to them. The results showed that 90% of respondents rated workshops as important or extremely important, with only 78% rated reading library science publications as important or extremely important, and 57% rated attending meetings of library associations as important or extremely important.

It is particularly interesting to note that in some ways the third most valued experience, attending professional association meetings, is very much like attending a workshop. This preference is not restricted to public library directors. In a study of its membership conducted in the spring of 1991, the Special Libraries Association concluded that two-thirds of its membership found the Association's professional development program a valuable service.

This survey also asked members to indicate their interest in five types of educational services: seminars (workshops), self-study courses, videotapes, audiotapes, and in-house training/seminars. The respondents provided the following rankings: 78% stated they would either definitely or probably attend an educational seminar, 52% expressed an interest in in-house training/seminars, and 43% expressed an interest in self-study. Though the self-study figure is high, it is still far behind workshops and in-house training, especially when you consider the fact that these two headings are similar, This preference for workshops is not new in the library profession.

In her landmark study of continuing education, Betty Stonu found that the three modes of continuing library education that received the highest use were attending professional meetings, participation in professional committees and attending workshops. When one looks at how these same respondents rated the effectiveness of these modes, however, the profession's preference for workshops is again indicated with 74% of respondents identifying the workshop as an effective means of continuing education, while only 57% found professional meetings an effective means, and committee work was found to be an effective continuing education vehicle by only 43%."

This preference for the workshop mode of continuing education is not limited to participants. Providers seem to prefer this mode as well. In a recent article in *Public Libraries*, a survey conducted by Blazek and Perrault indicated that 95% of responding state librarians viewed their institutions as having a responsibility for the continuing education of public library employees engaged in the provision of reference service. This same population indicated that the group workshop was the preferred means of addressing this need with the only exception being the evaluation of reference departments.

For this activity, state librarians preferred to use members of the library staff or contracted consultants. According to the *1992 Library and Information Science Education Statistical Report* the ALA-acre edited library schools in the United States and Canada held over 153 workshops in 1990-91. This is the most frequently used mode of continuing education provided by these schools. Other modes included colloquia/lectures (128), institutes/symposia/conferences (74), short courses (63), and seminars (58). All of these events are group activities that occur in an established, narrowly defined time period. They are in essence a sub-species of the genus workshop. In fact, the only two non-workshop formats on which data were collected are tutorials and other formats. In 1991, these formats only accounted for 10 activities. The library profession's continuing education ecology, therefore, is dominated by a mode that is "event-focused."

One of the most attractive features of the workshop as a continuing education mode is that it enables one to leave if not the library at least the desk at which one works. This is itself a good thing since it allows the participant to focus on the workshop topic in an environment that is more conducive to learning and also limits the day to day distractions that impede learning in the workplace. While these factors may contribute to a conducive learning environment and while they may increase the learning that goes on in the workshop, they also decrease the likelihood that this learning will be successfully integrated as part of the participant's day to day work life.

In their new book entitled *Transfer of Training*, Mary L. Broad and John W. Newstrom cite a study conducted by Timothy Baldwin and Kevin Ford. Baldwin and Ford analyzed the perceptions of human resource development professionals regarding the transfer of the content of management development programs. On the average, these professionals believed that only 40% of the content of programs they conducted was transferred to the work environment immediately after training, about 25% was still being applied six months later, and a mere 15% was still being used at the end of the year.

In their article, "Improving In service. Training' The Message of Research," Uruce Joyce anci IJeverly Showers provide achievement for workshops that work. These two authors examined over 200 studies on training effectiveness. Their conclusions are that in order for workshops to be effective they must incorporate a mixture of the following elements: presentation of theory and rationale, modeling or demonstration, practice under simulated conditions, structured feedback, and finally coaching in the use of the new skill or strategy.

To illustrate this point further, in a workshop where only theory and rationale are presented to participants, only 10 out of 100 participants will acquire the skills taught. In a workshop where participants receive both theory and rationale and have a number of opportunities to see the skill demonstrated, between 10 and 30 participants out of 100 will acquire the new skill. In a workshop where theory and rationale are presented and participants have a number of opportunities to see the skill demonstrated and get to practice the skills themselves with some feedback regarding their performance, between 80 and 90 participants out of 100 will acquire the skill.

One of the best examples of the use of this information in librarianship is the State of Maryland's reference training program. In 1983, the Division of Library Development and Services of the Maryland State Department of Education hired a survey research firm to conduct a massive, unobtrusive study of reference performance in Maryland. Librarians in Maryland were able to answer reference questions accurately only 55% of the time, a result that is in keeping with other studies conducted in other locations. What was unique about the Maryland study, however, was that not only was reference accuracy measured, but the behaviors which contributed to it were also identified. Based on the results of this study, the Division of Library Development and Services developed a three-day training program that incorporated all of the approaches mentioned by Joyce and Showers.

Librarians who received this training achieved 77% reference accuracy in a follow-up study while librarians who did not receive it only provided accurate answers 60% of the time. More importantly, in two locations staff not only participated in the three-day training program but engaged in intensive peer coaching and intermittent coaching and received supervisory support. In the follow-up study, the librarians in these two locations provided accurate answers to reference questions an average of 95% of the time." State-wide implementation of this training program resulted in a state-wide reference accuracy score of 65% in 1986 and 70% in 1990.

In addition to reassessing reference accuracy, the 1990 study also sought to determine which activities supported the continued use of behaviors that contribute to a complete and accurate answer. This aspect of the study was very important, since it was discovered that overall use of the model reference behaviors in the state had declined. This decline is consistent with what studies like those of Baldwin and Ford tell us about the effectiveness of workshop or event-oriented programs.

Activities that supported the continued use of the model reference behaviors were a training program or event that provided sufficient time for participants to learn and practice the behaviors, peer coaching several times a week for at least one month after the training, and specific strategies for maintaining the model reference behaviors such as a reference policy requiring their use. The study also pointed out that a combination of all three would have a significant impact on the continued use of these behaviors.

The Maryland reference training program is an exemplary program. Yet, as the cited studies show, this training program alone does not result in continued application of new skills on the job. In this specific case, however, a great deal of thought, time, energy, and commitment have gone into ensuring that the model reference behaviors do indeed transfer to the workplace. The Maryland program was developed by a group of individuals who were extremely knowledgeable about adult learning and the development of continuing education activities. It is unfortunate that these skills are not more widespread in the profession.

During 1991, the Continuing Library Education Network/Round Table (CLENE/RT) and the Southeastern Library Network (SOLINET) conducted a survey of continuing education providers in the southeastern United States. A total of 134 continuing education providers and staff development officers responded to this survey. The following was revealed: 72% of respondents devoted less than 25% of their time to continuing education and staff development; 32% of these individuals have 3 years or less experience with continuing education; and 31% of these individuals have a wide-range of continuing education responsibilities. This range is wide enough to indicate that these individuals have total program responsibility for continuing education and staff development in their organizations. For example, it was not unusual for an individual to indicate responsibility for managing, developing, coordinating, and supervising continuing education activities. In several cases, the respondents indicated that they also served as instructions in continuing education activities.

The individuals who responded to this survey were asked to participate in a focus-group sponsored by CLENE and SOLINET at the American Library Association's 1991 annual meeting in Atlanta. Approximately 30 individuals participated in this focus group, the purpose of which was to identify the continuing education needs of the region's continuing library educators. The top three needs identified by the participants were: assistance in identifying continuing education resources; continuing education program planning; and assistance in identifying needs assessment strategies and developing needs assessment competencies.

Based on the evidence offered thus far, one can only conclude that librarianship has a continuing education ecology that is fragile and endangered. The library profession's continuing education ecology is event-focused. These events occur in organizations which do not have strong transfer of training programs in place. It is also a system that is managed by individuals with limited experience in continuing education and who do not give a significant portion of their time to it. All of this adds up to a system that, at best, can be minimally effective in producing significant and lasting change, such as that urged in the three documents discussed earlier in this article.

How then does librarianship achieve its goal of repositioning itself to be the information profession in society? If the "new blood" approach will not work and our continuing education ecology is toxic, how are we to achieve significant and lasting change in librarianship? The profession must-to borrow a phrase from the 60s-change the system.

A GREEN MOVEMENT FOR THE PROFESSION

In her article, "Staff Development: Where Do We Go From Here?" Sheila Creth states that if she were conducting a performance evaluation for the library profession in staff development she would be inclined to give it a "C-" with many libraries deserving a failing grade and only a very few deserving an "A." This author certainly supports Creth's assessment. Several groups, however, are working to strengthen the profession's continuing education ecology.

The Association of Research Libraries through its Office of Management Services conducts a Training Skills Institute. This institute is designed to aid in the development of in-house training programs by developing the training competencies of its participants. The Library of Congress's Technical Processing and Automation Instruction Office has developed a 30-hour train-the-trainer program. This program was field-tested and evaluated at Simmons College during the spring of 1990.

The Library of Congress is currently revising this program and is considering offering it to the library community at large. Here again, this effort is aimed at strengthening the system by developing the talent that is latent within it. CLENE has also begun a long-range and strategic planning process whose purpose is to identify ways for CLENE to strengthen and support the profession's continuing education system.

Strengthening the existing system, however, will not be enough. In order to produce change of the magnitude contained in the *Statement on the Decade of the Librarian, Information 2000,* and *Strategic Visions for Professional*

Librarians, the profession needs to reorient its efforts. What is needed is a continuing education system that resembles the one described by Twain. This is one in which learning occurs at the point of practice; that uses the talents of experienced practitioners to educate and train new or inexperienced staff; and that develops a culture in which individuals assume responsibility for their own growth and the growth of their colleagues. What is needed is a system that embodies some of the principles advocated by the Green Movement.

The Greens are best known for their pro-environment policies. These polices are ultimately aimed at providing a safe and reasonable environment in which human beings can work and achieve fulfilling lives. Taking direction from the Greens, this article concludes with a framework for achieving a safe and reasonable environment in which librarians can work and achieve fulfilling lives. The proposed "Green Movement in Librarianship" would be based on the following principles:

1. Human beings are self-renewing resources.
2. Human beings require a safe, nurturing environment in which to renew themselves.
3. Organizations, agencies, policies or individuals who do not actively create safe and nurturing environments actively work against self-renewal. There is no neutral ground.
4. Each individual is responsible for his or her own renewal.
5. Each individual is responsible for the renewal of his or her colleagues.

The following strategies would form an action agenda for a Green Movement in the profession:

1. Librarians should become informed consumers of continuing education. Librarians should learn to

distinguish a good workshop from a bad one. Librarians should provide specific feedback to providers about what worked and what did not, what was helpful and what would be more helpful.

2. Efforts to develop competent and highly skilled continuing education practitioners in librarianship should be increased and expanded.

3. Transfer of training strategies should be in place in the profession. All elements of the system-participants, supervisors, employing organizations, trainers and sponsoring organizations-must assume responsibility for ensuring that training does indeed transfer.

4. Continuing education in the profession must be moved as close to the point of practice as possible.

This is not a fully developed program. It is proposed simply as a means to begin the discussion of what a Green Movement in librarianship might look like and what actions it might take. The intended outcome of such a movement, however, is fully developed. The outcome of such a movement would be the creation of a self-renewing profession. In essence, this movement would advance librarianship from being a learned profession to becoming a learning one.

Staff training and development is a key area for any librarian or information manager. For the service to operate effectively, library and information staff need to be seen not merely as signposts to sources, but rather as the key to their effective use and exploitation, that is, as professional information handlers and organizers who are also good communicators.

Today's multimedia information-dependent society presents numerous opportunities for those working in LIS to be involved in a range of activities across the organization in which they work. For example, the information department of a legal or accounting practice could easily be involved in a range of IT (information technology) developments across the firm, such as the setting up of internal databases and records management systems, as well as in other company-wide activities such as marketing and PR. In public libraries there has been a considerable increase in the setting up of new or specialist services and departments, for example the introduction of public-access IT-based services such as OPACs or CD-ROMs; or of fee-based business information services. In both these examples, attitudes and skills as well as specialist knowledge are crucial.

There are also services which operate off-site, taking information out to particular areas of the community, for example to prisons or to the house bound. Both private sector companies and local authorities are being called upon to streamline procedures and become more cost-effective, introducing mure value-added services, for which charges are increasingly likely to be made to the ultimate user of the information. All these activities require a variety of skills and knowledge over and above basic information-seeking and finding skills - which are in themselves becoming more complex, yet at the same time more exciting given the range of sources and formats now available, including the ability to manipulate data as well as store it.

Already the few examples given above will have indicated numerous possible areas for training and development, but in addition to skills and knowledge there is another vital objective: that of raising staff morale and motivation, something which underpins the whole service. If morale is low and motivation lacking in just one member of staff, it quickly reflects on the service as a whole.

All types of library and information service benefit from the encouragement and support of training and development, but it must be carefully planned and structured, and available to staff at all levels. Before going any further it might be useful to mention the difference between training and development, although they are closely linked. Training is usually considered to be the process through which job-related skills are achieved, yet at the same time it is itself part of the broader process of an individual's development, the latter being concerned with attitudes, motivation, increased awareness and personal qualities. Training could perhaps be regarded as a series of short clearly defined modules, whereas development is a lifelong process contributing to personal as well as work-related advancement.

Each time a new member of staff is appointed, a new personality with a variety of experience, knowledge, interests and skills is brought into the organization. As the departmental manager you will want to help that person to build on those, and in so doing, enhance both the service and the job. However, your involvement will not only benefit the individual and the service: the process of training and developing your staff will also be instrumental in your own personal development.

Libraries and information services operate within a whole range of organizational settings: they may be part of a public library service within a local authority or form a central part of the educational process, for example within a university. Government departments, both central and local, also have large collections of information, as do hospitals, charities and voluntary organizations, industrial and commercial firms, professional and trade associations. The organizational objectives may be very different, as may be the way in which information is used and perceived.

Different information needs may be satisfied in different ways, but there will be certain core areas of information organization and handling which will be common to all. The key factors likely to dictate the direction and style of information provision and exploitation are, first, the objectives that need to be met by the organization, and secondly, the organizational culture, for example the hierarchy, structure, norms and procedures that exist. These will all need to be considered when setting out to establish a training and development policy for the library or information department, which may itself be part of another broader function such as research or education. This is quite common in the private sector, as demonstrated in a research study which looked at 65 business organizations and revealed that in almost half of them LIS formed part of another department - marketing, computer services, research or consultancy.

It could also be the case that the LIS has other functions as part of its overall portfolio; for example, information services may include responsibility for records management, database development or IT training. Having talked about such diversity in terms of the private sector, it must be said that there are just as many different LIS roles in the public sector, for example in public libraries there are youth libraries, music and drama collections, local history archives, reference, business and commercial services.

Another notable difference between public libraries and special libraries is that in the public library setting the organization will have within it a large number of library/ information staff, whereas in an industrial or commercial firm, however large the library/information service may be, the LIS staff will always be very much in a minority.

This is something of which the manager needs to be very aware in terms of the possible differences in organizational understanding and perception of the capability of LIS staff, and the way in which that could influence support for their training and development. This therefore forms a key part of the development process that managers themselves need to pursue, i.e. acquiring an understanding of the organization and the skills to ensure that understanding is put to maximum use in developing the full potential of the individual and the service to meet the organization's objectives.

All these factors will influence the type of training activity that you will want and need to put into place, and the personal qualities that individuals will require to be effective in their particular role. Throughout Part Two current practice is illustrated by case studies. Examples quoted from management and professional literature are also used to demonstrate ways in which training and development activities can be structured and mantiged. Case studies include international, national and locally based organizations. The first of these shows the importance of integrating specialist training into the organization's overall training programme.

CASE STUDY: THE BRITISH COUNCIL

The British Council, when planning training for its library and information staff, literally has to think globally, having around 90 offices and 6500 staff in countries throughout the world. The aim of the British Council is to promote Britain abroad and to provide access to British ideas, talents and experience in education and training, books and periodicals, the English language, the arts, the sciences and technology.

Among its services each office provides a library and information service to local enquirers seeking answers to questions about almost anything to do with life in Britain, with a considerable number of these enquirers seeking details about various aspects of British education. Enquiries may come from government offices, local universities and other organizations, or from interested individuals. The Libraries Books and Information Division (LIBID) at the headquarters of the British Council in Manchester is responsible for designing and running a series of specific training events for different levels of LIS staff, covering a range of subjects and using a variety of teaching methods and materials. However, the development of training for all divisions is carried out in conjunction with the central training department and as part of the British Council's overall management and development programme, MANDATE.

MANDATE was introduced in 1991 and staff were familiarized with the concept through the circulation of a well set-out leaflet describing the programme and its benefits. Sections of this are reproduced below with kind permission of the British Council.

What is Mandate?

- Mandate stands for Management Training and Development Exercise
- Mandate provides training and development services required by managers and their staff to achieve corporate objectives
- Mandate's services are shaped by the Council's priorities
- Mandate gives you the opportunity to improve your skills and develop your career

What are the Benefits?

Mandate benefits you, your line manager and the Council because it:

- meets direct needs and is job-related
- fosters personal development and professionalism
- gives a sense of direction to training and development
- increases effectiveness and efficiency
- improves communication
- improves morale
- supports key changes
- gives an organizational focus to development
- attracts and keeps good staff

How Mandate Helps You

- The programmes are developmental: you are able to undertake further training in key skills as you move jobs or through the grades
- The programmes are flexible: you do the training when you and your line manager feel that you need it
- The programmes are innovative and you learn in many different ways: open learning, courses and workshops, computer-based training, projects, attachments and job-swaps
- The training modules will be offered regularly in the UK and in two designated Regional Training Centres in Egypt and India

Other Services that Mandate provides

- Specialist advice to help line managers identify training needs and strategies
- Specific training for work units and projects
- Full-time or short-term external training where appropriate
- Customized Professional Training Programmes (for individuals or groups) to update specialist knowledge and skills
- A Management Qualifications Programme using distance learning and leading to the Certificate or Diploma in Management
- Training for trainers: those who have responsibility in work units for training other staff
- A Further Education Scheme to support personal development, particularly for junior staff

- Language training and cultural orientation to prepare UK staff for an overseas posting

[The leaflet also shows the core Mandate programmes with a chart grouping the training modules by skill area and type of course, the names of the training team responsible for each type of programme, and a list of the specialist training and development advisers who have been assigned to each division.]

The Libraries Books and Information Division (LIBID) runs a number of specialist programmes for staff worldwide, some with English as a first language and many with a different mother tongue; both with and without US qualifications. The subjects covered range from book promotion and information provision to information technology and library and information services management. Course development has been very much as a response to feedback, particularly from overseas participants who have attended previous courses. Details are circulated to all offices worldwide and course descriptions, especially in terms of the aims and level, have to be clearly stated in order that those wishing to apply have all the information necessary to help them make the most appropriate choice.

Because of the complexity of getting people from around the world together for a course, training events have to be planned well in advance and programmes scheduled to allow overseas visitors to take the opportunity to arrange other commitments during their stay. Those running British Council courses need to take particular account of cultural differences, for example the accepted use and form of personal names, and special learning requirements of delegates e.g. in terms of language. Training materials, especially handouts and work- books, play an important part, offering delegates the chance to re-read those sections of the programme where they require better understanding, and giving them something to take back to the workplace for future reference.

This first chapter and the case study illustrate the numerous considerations for any LIS manager seeking to review the training and development opportunities for, and needs of, their staff. It also emphasizes the benefits to both the individual and the service of viewing such activities in an organizational context.

STAFF DEVELOPMENT IN 1990'S

Some of the human resource management issues that face academic and research libraries are specific to librarianship and reside on a macro or profession-wide level. Recruitment of talented, qualified individuals to the profession, adequate pay for the level of knowledge and skill required by library work, and the nature of library education are three examples. For the most part, libraries and library staff compensate for the results of these broader problems by developing local initiatives. Until all the stakeholders agree to some form of collective action, library administrators and their staff will have to continue to mitigate their effects through individual efforts. One definition of human resource management is "that area of organization life that focuses on the effective management and utilization of people."

This function is often understood to mean administrative activities such as recruitment, wage and payroll management, and benefits. Over the past forty years, however, a shift in the concept of management from control to development has led to a more inclusive definition of the human resources field. With a growing recognition of the key role staff play in the success of an organization, it now encompasses those activities that promote greater job satisfaction and that support the development of individuals within the context of the workplace. Academic and research libraries generally have good programs and structures to manage the administrative aspects of a human resource program either because it is good management practice or because they are part of a larger institution that is required by law to do so. Libraries tend to have weaker programs and structures in human resources development areas, such as training and staff development and formal programs that lead to organizational renewal. Part of the problem is that human resource management and development has not been recognized as a priority in academic and research libraries, and it has been underfunded in the past. The practice has been to spend the lion's share of resources on fulfilling patron needs through the acquisition of more and better collections and services.

Investment in the improvement of the library's ability as an organization or its staffs ability as individuals to fulfill those needs is not a strategy that has been widely pursued. As a result, organizational and profession-wide infrastructures are not in place to meet current needs for human resource management and development, much less those that are anticipated.

HUMAN RESOURCE MANAGEMENT AND DEVELOPMENT PROGRAMS

Shelley Phipps, Associate Director for Science Libraries at (he University of Arizona, reminds "that we are serving people in the educational process, we are linking people in the knowledge development process, and we are ultimately dependent on people to achieve progress in our efforts to improve and enhance access, storage, and preservation of the knowledge base." Academic and research libraries and their staff face many challenges, including ongoing funding difficulties and anticipated changes in technology, demographics, and the flow of scholarly communication. Well-conceived programs and well-designed structures will be needed to improve and upgrade organizational capabilities and staff skills as these changes occur. Some of the initiatives will be organizationally based and others will relate to improving personal or role effectiveness. The key human resource development issues will need to be addressed either through the creation of new programs or by making improvements to existing ones.

ORGANIZATIONAL INITIATIVES

From an organizational point of view, academic and research libraries have, for the most part, created effective structures for managing the administrative aspects of this function. Most of the libraries that are members of the Association of Research Libraries (ARL) have an individual, often either a librarian or personnel professional, designated to manage and act as liaison with the university or host institution for activities such as recruitment, payroll, and benefits.

Key organizational issues for the 1990s will revolve around the development of comprehensive human resource programs, the design and implementation of flexible, responsive organizational structures, and the nurturing of organizational cultures to sustain them.

Planning for Human Resource Management and Development

One key area of weakness in the human resource management process in academic and research libraries has been planning. Planning is a relatively new phenomenon for these libraries in general. Over the years, a number of studies have shown that, for a variety of reasons, academic and research libraries have not engaged in planning processes that would permit them to set goals, measure performance, and develop strategies for improvement. This appears to be changing as more libraries engage in strategic planning.

Business and industry have applied planning processes to human resource management both as a way of anticipating and responding to external forces and as a means of understanding and dealing with existing and emerging internal needs. To stay competitive, these organizations pay close attention to matching staffing levels with production and/or service goals and opportunities. This is obviously much more problematic for libraries that cannot generate more revenue even when an emerging need requiring more staff is identified.

In an era of shrinking resources, when libraries anticipate having to make choices among the many services and programs they would like to offer, rational human resource planning can be a valuable tool in the decision-making process. Carefully collected data and clearly conceived rationale will go a long way to helping garner stakeholder support when programs have to be terminated.

Performance planning, career planning, and training and development planning can be used to improve the effectiveness of existing staff. Establishing mutually developed goals and objectives can serve as a powerful communication device between the organization and the staff and between the manager and employee. They clarify direction and expectations, and they provide a mechanism for improvement. If a gap between goal and performance is seen as an opportunity for improvement rather than for punishment, planning, as embodied in the goal and objective setting process, provides a powerful organizational and individual learning device.

To make the most of the money available for training and staff development, careful planning is also required. William Tracey, a leading expert in the area of training systems design, recommends a systems approach. This process begins with an analysis of needs and the collection of job data. Objectives and evaluative measures clarify the goals of the program. Materials, programs and participants are chosen based on the degree to which they fulfill the overall mission and goals of the organization, A systematic approach facilitates the level of accountability that is increasingly an expectation for not-for-profit organizations.

Organizational Structures

There are a number of ways to design a structure for an organization. The most common are either to use the industry standard, i.e., what everyone else uses, or to use a standard form, such as a pyramid hierarchy or teams. The shape of academic and research libraries as organizations is generally taken for granted.

A new academic or research library is so seldom created that there is little experience with an organizational design process that matches the work that needs to be done with the most effective structure. Because every program or service already has its own constituency, there has also been a reluctance and resistance to questioning the need to continue an existing set of activities. As a result, reorganizations generally focus on moving an operation from one group to another.

With economic constraints as a feature for the foreseeable future, the pressure increases to question what an academic or research library does, how it does it, and for whom. This provides an opportunity for these libraries to rethink how they will organize staff and other resources in support of user needs. As more libraries engage in this process, a beginning point should be involving the people who do the work. It both takes advantage of the intelligence, energy, and expertise of staff and strengthens their commitment to the workplace.

The most important part of this rethinking process, however, will be the creation of structures that are capable of being selfrenewing. With the rate of change that is anticipated, aligning tasks, goals, technology, communication needs, problem-solving needs, and decision-making requirements will require ongoing attention. Programs and services will have to be reviewed continually for relevance, and the organizational resources assigned to them reallocated as needs change. With staff as a resource, individuals will also have to he prepared to be redeployed. This will require a major shift in the way the staff think about their relationships to their jobs and to the organization for which they work. It will also require an increased commitment to retraining.

ORGANIZATIONAL CULTURE

The "culture" of an organization can be defined as "a pattern of basic assumptions-invented, discovered, or developed by a given group as it learns to cope with its problems of external adaptation and internal integration ... taught to new members as the correct way to perceive, think, and feel in relation to those problems."

Culture is the basic system of values and beliefs that underlie and guide the choices and decisions that individuals in an organization make. Because it has generally not been discussed, it goes unrecognized as a force. It is often unclear why we do certain things other than because "that's how we do things here" or "we've always done it that way here."

Cultures can be built and supported in many different ways. One of the first opportunities libraries have to influence the thinking of staff is the orientation program. This program should go beyond a recitation of benefits and an overview of the departments of the library. If the library does not use this opportunity to begin instilling a sense of overall mission and purpose, then the employee is more vulnerable to the point of view of a counterproductive subculture.

Symbolic actions are a strong force in shaping culture. These may take the form of rituals that underscore the values of the organization as well as forms of relaxation that support a sense of community. Some of the symbolic activities in which libraries engage are staff award ceremonies, the use of the staff newsletter to recognize the achievements of an individual or a department, and annual meetings with the director. Playfulness can provide a different kind of opportunity for building culture. Summer barbecues, Christmas parties, and regular events like an annual bowling contest or skating outing become the means for strengthening relationships that must operate well in the workplace.

The role of culture has become more of an issue as academic and research libraries reexamine their mission and how they will fulfill it. The values and beliefs that support a collection-based library may not be the same as those needed to support an access-based one. Libraries that recognize such a key change will need to "manage" their cultures. This will require a clear understanding of what the culture supports and what it defends against. After comparing the current culture with what is needed to support the movement toward a desired future, attention will need to be paid to fostering a set of desired values and beliefs.

STAFF SKILLS INITIATIVES

It is important that programs focusing on an individual's ability to operate effectively in the work environment be seen as a partnership, a joint responsibility of the library and the individual involved. Human resource initiatives that focus on the individual need to be divided into two categories: those that focus on supervisors and managers, and those that relate to staff as individual members of their organizational community.

The Challenges to Managers

In their recent book on the workforce in the year 2000, Loden and Rosener suggest that "developing cooperative and committed work groups in which diversity is respected and supported will lie a major task for corporate society during the next decade." This will be no less true for academic and not-for-profit organizations. The three key words or phrases in this statement are developing, work group and diversity. They pinpoint the strategic issues for librarians and library staff with management and supervisory responsibility in the 1990s.

Even in the most enlightened of management models, managers and supervisors have relied on control as a means of "accomplishing work through others," the traditional definition of management. Control might have taken the form of autocratic or prescriptive behavior as it was practiced in early bureaucratic organizations, or it might be participatory as it is seen today in organizations that recognize the benefits of jointly-developed goals and objectives. In the end, however, control models rely on policies, rules, rewards, punishments, and oversight of work to ensure a satisfactory level of performance.

In a period of shrinking resources, "satisfactory" performance is no longer enougli. Every library needs the wholehearted effort of each employee to get everything done that needs to get done. The question library managers are facing is how to obtain that level of performance. Some of the most effective strategies appear to he those that focus on developing employee commitment to results by increasing a personal sense of ownership. Some of the strategies being used are: involving staff in organizational planning, problem-solving and decision-making through teams and groups, profit- sharing and pay for performance strategies, and self-managed work groups.

Some of these strategies are relatively unavailable to academic and research libraries, such as profit-sharing and pay-for-performance. A few libraries have begun to experiment with organizational strategies, including the development of collateral structures that permit staff to participate in organizational planning and decision-making, and with self-managed teams.

Coaching is one of the most powerful tools for the individual manager or supervisor in improving performance. It is through this process that the employee can learn how to learn and develops the kind of commitment to personal development that leads to continuous improvement. Through regular, one-on-one conversations with a staff member, a manager can help the individual develop problem-solving skills, increase their sensitivity to organizational issues and constraints, improve technical competence, and identify the means for improved performance.

Libraries are using many kinds of groups in the workplace, both to improve personal satisfaction and to improve organizational problem-solving. Library staff are often expected to participate in both short-term task forces with a specific task to accomplish and their primary work groups to which they contribute on an ongoing basis. The need for library managers and supervisors, as well as individual library staff, to be adept at working with groups will become more critical in the future. With the increased expectation of participation in the workplace and the increased complexity of problems requiring diverse points of view for solution, groups will become evermore a fact of organizational life.

Because an enormous amount of time and effort is spent in working with groups in libraries, it is critical that adequate preparation be provided to those who are expected to manage these groups. Arthur Van Gundy, a researcher in the area of group problem-solving, suggests three primary areas that require training for optimal group performance.

First, a group leader must know how to assess and use resources possessed by a group. Participants in a group may be chosen for a variety of reasons, and it is important to be aware of the nature of the contribution each can make to the process. Secondly, a group leader is responsible for establishing a climate where the creative potential of the group can emerge. Third, they must know how to structure the process, so that each member can play a productive role in the process. Training programs need to be established in libraries that make available training to staff who are expected to play this kind of leadership position in groups whether as a onetime or ongoing assignment.

In their book, *Managing the Workforce 2000*, David Jamieson and Julie O'Mara suggest that as diversity in the workforce grows, another key to improving performance will be individualizing the performance management in a way that "will awaken people to their individual strengths and unique perspectives." As managers who have begun to work actively at developing skills that empower others already know, this will pose an ongoing challenge. This approach requires sensitivity and balance among the needs of the individual, the group, and the library as a whole. It is an approach that encourages change, and the manager who facilitates this process needs both training and organizational support to operate effectively in an environment with these expectations.

Developing the Individual

There are three areas that will require close attention by libraries creating human resource development programs tailored for the individual staff member: technology skills, interpersonal skills, and leadership.

"The human element is the critical facilitator or bottleneck to effective use of IT" (information technology). To integrate effectively new technologies into the library, much more needs to be invested in technology training and education. Technology training means teaching people to use both the equipment and the software when they are needed to support or improve personal or organizational effectiveness. The time and energy of staff are too expensive to permit individuals to learn and make mistakes on their own. Systematic programs that ensure consistent use of compatible programs will be required to manage the fast pace of technological obsolescence and change.

Technology education is a broader concept that implies understanding of the conceptual framework in which technology exists, so that the individual can make intelligent decisions about when and how to employ it. While most system-wide decisions are made at the management level, staff have a valuable role to play in identifying needs and areas that could be improved through automation and other applications of technology. As with any other change in the workplace, staff participation in these kinds of decisions will make changes that much easier to accomplish.

Increasing interdependence and diversity in the workplace will require a greater level of skill in interpersonal relations in the future. Individual staff members will need to be capable of accepting and confronting differences without the constant mediation of a manager or supervisor. As members of groups, library staff will need to learn how to use their individual strengths to contribute most effectively to a decision-making or problem-solving session. The more interdependent work becomes, the more staff will have to rely on collaborative skills as a means of working with and influencing others.

These are skills, not necessarily naturally occurring traits. If library management expects staff to exhibit them in the workplace, then it has a responsibility to hire staff with these skills, to support those who have them, and to help those who may not have them to build competency in using them.

The concept of leadership is also changing, so that it is no longer the sole purview of managers and administrators. As society begins to move beyond the concept of "heroic leadership," individual staff members will need to consider their personal responsibility for meaningful, creative change in the workplace. If libraries are to be successful into the next century, the work of thinking and acting positively about the future and setting constructive goals will need to be the responsibility of all members of the workplace community. Efforts must be made to encourage and support staff to play a significant role in articulating and establishing an optimistic agenda for the future of libraries.

FLEXIBILITY AND LEARNING

The greatest challenge that faces academic and research libraries, librarians, and staff is the ability to function effectively in a changing environment. Most people understand this to mean controlling change. There are indeed strategies that an organization or an individual can use to outline a change process to ensure a smooth transition from one form of operation to another.

Much of the change that occurs today, however, and most of the change that is likely to occur in the future, is imposed. It is change that originates elsewhere; it is change over which an individual or even an institution can exert little control.

The last twenty years have given us a taste of life in a world of rapid, continuous change. The one thing upon which futurists and experts in every field can agree is that this turbulent discontinuity in our environment will continue well into the next century. It means that, rather than preparing for something in particular, organizations and individuals must simply, like a boy or girl scout, "Be prepared."

For libraries and library staff, being "prepared" will mean being flexible and capable of shifting quickly in response to changing conditions. They will have to learn how to make decisions and choices in the present about an unknown future. To accomplish this, a willingness to take risks and a positive personal and organizational attitude toward learning will have to be integrated into the value systems and into the cultures of these libraries. On an organizational and individual level, learning how to learn from both successful and unsuccessful initiatives will be a critical factor in the survival and success of this profession and its institutions.

Conclusion

ARL represents the 119 largest academic and research libraries in the United States and Canada. On average, salary and wages represent 50% of their operating budgets, As an aggregate, this equals approximately $460,000,000. Given anticipated ongoing funding difficulties, it is critical that libraries get the best possible value from this major investment. Library schools prepare professionals by providing them with a theoretical framework and the basic knowledge and skills to support the mission and tasks of the library as it currently exists and as it has existed in the past. Library staff come into libraries with a wide variety of backgrounds, experiences, and skills. In order to ensure continuing success, these knowledge and skill bases will have to be constantly updated as the nature of (he work and the library as an institution change. This will require both financial resources for continuing education and development, and a sense of personal responsibility for learning and renewal. A much larger investment in staff training and development and in organizational development will be necessary to create and support the value systems and cultures required to meet the challenges of the twenty-first century.